Writing Prompts for Teens

Quick, Fun, and Easy Prompts to Spark Ideas and Build Writing Confidence in Minutes

DR. FANATOMY

GIFT FOR TEEN

copyright@ dr. fanatomy 2025

All rights reserved. No part of this publication may be reproduced, distributed, or transmitted in any form or by any means, including photocopying, recording, or other electronic or mechanical methods, without the prior written permission of the publisher, except in the case of brief quotations embodied in critical reviews and certain other noncommercial uses permitted by copyright law.

This book is a work of non-fiction, and any resemblance to actual persons, living or dead, or actual events is purely coincidental.

The information and techniques described in this book are intended for educational and informational purposes only. The author and publisher shall not be held liable for any injury, damage, or loss arising from using or misusing the information presented in this book.

While every effort has been made to ensure the accuracy of the information contained within this book, the author and publisher make no warranties or representations express or implied, about the completeness, accuracy, reliability, suitability, or availability with respect to the contents of this book for any purpose. The use of any information provided in this book is at the reader's own risk.

copyright@ dr. fanatomy 2025

All rights reserved. No part of this publication may be reproduced, distributed, or transmitted in any form or by any means, including photocopying, recording, or other electronic or mechanical methods, without the prior written permission of the publisher, except in the case of brief quotations embodied in critical reviews and certain other noncommercial uses permitted by copyright law.

This book is a work of non-fiction, and any resemblance to actual persons, living or dead, or actual events is purely coincidental.

The information and techniques described in this book are intended for educational and informational purposes only. The author and publisher shall not be held liable for any injury, damage, or loss arising from using or misusing the information presented in this book.

While every effort has been made to ensure the accuracy of the information contained within this book, the author and publisher make no warranties or representations express or implied, about the completeness, accuracy, reliability, suitability, or availability with respect to the contents of this book for any purpose. The use of any information provided in this book is at the reader's own risk.

TABLE OF CONTENTS

BOOK INTRODUCTION: SPARK YOUR CREATIVITY IN MINUTES
(Pg:3-10)

- Your Journey Starts Here
- Why This Book? Quick Prompts to Build Your Writing Confidence
- Your Confidence-Building Roadmap
- Mindmap: Your Creative Journey
- Why This Makes the Perfect Teen Gift
- How to Use This Book: Easy, Fun, and Pressure-Free
- Warm-Up Exercises and sample answers

CHAPTER 1: OWN YOUR IDEAS - QUICK MINDSET SHIFTS FOR CONFIDENCE
(Pg: 11-23)

- Unlocking Teen Creativity Fast
- Prompts #1-17: Identity Sparks
- Your Identity Vibe Flowchart
- Building Confidence with Fun Sparks
- Prompts #18-35: Confidence Boosters
- Quiz: Creativity Quick Check
- Prompts #36-52: Idea Leaps
- Big Idea Energy Flowchart
- Activity Zone and Answers

CHAPTER 2: DAILY SPARKS - EASY HABITS FOR NON-STOP IDEAS
(Pg: 24-35)

- Making Writing Quick & Fun Every Day
- Table: Easy Setup Ideas
- Workflow: 10-Minute Idea Setup
- Prompts #53-69: Habit Starters
- Flowchart: Your Daily Vibe
- Turning Prompts into Play

TABLE OF CONTENTS

- Exercise: Habit Connector
- Prompts #70-87: Social Sparks
- Exercise: Mini-Share Boost
- Prompts #88-104: Friend-Focused Sparks
- Flowchart: Squad Vibe
- Activity Zone and Answers

CHAPTER 3: CRUSH WRITER'S BLOCK - FAST, FUN FIXES IN MINUTES
(Pg: 36-47)

- Spotting & Sparking Past Blocks
- Table: Triggers & Fixes
- Workflow: Instant Block Buster
- Prompts #105-121: Fast Sparks
- Flowchart: Block Buster Vibes
- Play to Spark Confidence
- Exercise: Idea Dump & Quick Shape
- Prompts #122-139: Playful Sparks
- Quiz: Block Buster Type
- Prompts #140-156: Recovery Sparks
- Monthly Check-In #3: Quick Reflection Grid
- Activity Zone and Answers

CHAPTER 4: IDEA PLAYGROUND - FUN GENRE SPARKS FOR EVERY MOOD
(Pg: 48-60)

- Fantasy & Sci-Fi Quick Adventures
- Mindmap: Epic Adventure Vibe
- Prompts #157-173: Fantasy & Sci-Fi Sparks
- Everyday Sparks & Emotions
- Exercise: Routine-to-Magic

TABLE OF CONTENTS

- Table: Character Depth Booster
- Exercise: Chat Boost
- Mindmap: Plot Pop Flow
- Prompts #279-296: Plot & Dialogue Sparks
- Quiz: Idea Power Check
- Prompts #297-313: Full Story Sparks
- Monthly Check-In #6: Quick Reflection Grid
- Activity Zone and Answers

CHAPTER 5: SPARK YOUR VOICE - EASY WAYS TO SOUND LIKE YOU

(Pg: 61-73)

- Why Your Voice Builds Confidence
- Table: Voice Spark Builder
- Workflow: Voice Quick Lab
- Prompts #210-226: Voice Sparks
- Risk Sparks & Bold Ideas
- Exercise: Bold Idea Try
- Prompts #227-244: Style Mixes
- Quiz: Voice Confidence Boost
- Prompts #245-261: Share-Ready Sparks
- Monthly Check-In #5: Quick Reflection Grid
- Activity Zone and Answers

CHAPTER 6: MAKE IDEAS POP - FUN STORY SPARKS IN MINUTES

(Pg:74-85)

- Ideas to Quick Stories
- Table: Character Spark Creator
- Workflow: Story Quick Map
- Mindmap: Story Vibe Flow

TABLE OF CONTENTS

- Prompts #262-278: Character Sparks
- Capturing Holiday Magic in Verse
- Table: Why Holiday Poetry Slays
- Christmas and Winter Wonders
- Table: Christmas and Winter Wonders
- Thanksgiving and Gratitude
- Prompt Practice: Holiday Glow
- Visual Tool: Holiday Prompt Planner
- Your Turn: Reflective Journal Page
- Visual Tool: Holiday Connection Mind Map
- Activity Zone and Answers

CHAPTER 7: SHARE WITH CONFIDENCE - EASY SPARKS TO GO PUBLIC

(Pg: 86-98)

- From Notebook to Quick Shares
- Table: Share Spot Guide
- Workflow: Confidence Share Plan
- Prompts #314-330: Share Sparks
- Table: Share Style Booster
- Writing as Endless Fun
- Prompts #331-348: Online Sparks
- Quiz: Confidence Spark Quiz
- Prompts #349-365: Pro Shares
- Table: Pro Share Booster
- Monthly Check-In #7: Quick Reflection Grid
- Activity Zone and Answers

CHAPTER 8: BOOK CONCLUSION: CELEBRATE YOUR CONFIDENCE GLOW-UP

(Pg: 99 -104)

- Your Year of Idea Sparks

TABLE OF CONTENTS

- Table: Year-End Spark Grid
- Exercise: 365th Spark Party
- Next Sparks: Your Writing Adventure
- Example: Teen Spark Mash-Up
- Quiz: Journey Spark Recap
- Sample Answer
- Table: Next Adventure Booster
- Final Reflection: Your Creative Glow-Up

APPENDIX (Pg: 105-107)

- Appendix -A: Creative Journey Tracker
- Appendix -B: Spark Mix-and-Match Planner
- Appendix - C: Share Style Toolkit

Spark Your Creativity in Minutes 🎉

Your Journey Starts Here

Hey, you! Yeah, you—the teen with a million ideas buzzing in your head, ready to light up the world! Welcome to 365 Writing Prompts for Teens: Quick, Fun, and Easy Prompts to Spark Ideas and Build Writing Confidence in Minutes. This book isn't just a journal—it's your ticket to turning random thoughts into epic stories, viral TikToks, or even the next big Netflix series idea, all in just 5 minutes a day! No stress, no boring lectures, just pure creative vibes. Ready to dive in? Let's make your ideas POP! 🚀

Why This Book? Quick Prompts to Build Your Writing Confidence
The Magic of Daily 5-Minute Writing ✨

Writing doesn't have to feel like homework or a TikTok trend you can't keep up with. This book provides 365 quick and fun prompts to spark your imagination, boost your confidence, and help you feel like a total creative rockstar. Think of it like a daily vibe check for your brain—5 minutes to jot down ideas, dream big, and flex your storytelling muscles. No pressure, just you being awesome.

Why it's dope:
- **Sparks Ideas Fast:** Each prompt is like a match lighting up your creativity. Stuck? Not anymore!
- **Builds Confidence:** Every word you write makes you bolder, whether it's a poem, a story, or a viral tweet.
- **Stress-Free Vibes:** No rules, no grades—just fun prompts that fit into your busy life.

Your Confidence-Building Roadmap 🎈
This book is your guide to becoming a writing legend, one quick prompt at a time. Here's a sneak peek at what's coming:

Chapter	Focus	Skills You'll Nail	Sample Prompt
1: Own Your Ideas	Creative mindset	Confidence, owning your voice	"You're a video game hero—what's your victory line?"
2: Daily Sparks	Building habits	Consistency, fun routines	"Your phone unlocks a time-travel app—what happens?"

Chapter	Focus	Skills You'll Nail	Sample Prompt
3: Crush Writer's Block	Beating creative slumps	Problem-solving, playfulness	"Write a silly rhyme to kickstart a story."
4: Idea Playground	Exploring genres	Imagination, storytelling	"Your crush is a secret spy—what's their mission?"
5: Spark Your Voice	Finding your style	Unique voice, bold expression	"Turn your life into a sarcastic comedy scene."
6: Make Ideas Pop	Crafting stories	Plot, characters, dialogue	"A flawed teen hero—what's their diary entry?"
7: Share with Confidence	Going public	Sharing, bravery	"Pitch your year-end story for a contest."

Mindmap: Your Creative Journey

(Imagine this as a colorful doodle in your notebook!)

Center: "Your Writing Glow-Up"

- Branch 1: Confidence → "Own your ideas" → Ch.1
- Branch 2: Daily Fun → "Quick habits" → Ch.2
- Branch 3: No Blocks → "Beat slumps" → Ch.3
- Branch 4: Epic Worlds → "Genres" → Ch.4
- Branch 5: Your Vibe → "Unique voice" → Ch.5
- Branch 6: Stories → "Plots & chars" → Ch.6
- Branch 7: Share It → "Go viral" → Ch.7

Why This Makes the Perfect Teen Gift 🎁

- Quick & Fun: 5-minute prompts fit into your crazy schedule.
- Confidence Booster: Feel like a creative boss with every word.

- **Year-Long Vibes:** 365 prompts = a full year of inspiration.
- **Perfect for Everyone:** Whether you love TikTok, gaming, or daydreaming, this book's got your vibe.
- **Stress Slasher:** Writing becomes your chill zone, not a chore.

Example Prompt: Your Life as a Movie Trailer 🎬

Prompt #1: "If your life was a movie trailer, what's the epic hook that grabs everyone's attention?"

Assignment: Write a 50-word trailer script that screams you. Think big—action, drama, or comedy vibes!

Sample Answer:
"In a world of chaos, one teen rises. Cue [Your Name], dodging school stress, gaming like a pro, and chasing dreams. With one epic moment—a viral TikTok dance—everything changes. 'This is my story,' they declare. Coming soon to a life near you!" (50 words)

Quick Tip: Picture your trailer with a dope soundtrack—maybe Billie Eilish or Post Malone? Make it you!

How to Use This Book: Easy, Fun, and Pressure-Free 😎

Workflow: 5-Minute Idea Spark ⚡

Here's how to make every prompt a creative win in just 5 minutes:
1. **Pick a Prompt:** Flip to today's number or choose one that vibes with you.
2. **Jot Ideas (3 mins):** Scribble whatever pops into your head—no overthinking!
3. **Reflect Quickly:** What's cool about what you wrote? Jot one thought.
4. **Build On It:** Save it, tweak it, or turn it into a TikTok idea later.

Visual Workflow
Start → [Pick Prompt] → [Write 3 mins] → [Quick Reflect] → [Save or Share] → Next Day!

Quiz: Find Your Creative Vibe 🎨

ake this quick quiz to discover your writing style and where to start in this book! (Picture this with fun emojis and check-boxes!)

1. What's your dream story vibe?
    - A) Epic fantasy with dragons 🐉
    - B) Real-life drama with tea 🍵
    - C) Sci-fi with cool tech 🤖
    - D) Funny TikTok-style skits 😆
2. What's your go-to app?
    - A) Wattpad for stories 📚
    - B) Instagram for aesthetics 📷
    - C) TikTok for trends 🎬
    - D) Gaming apps like Roblox 🎮
3. What scares you about writing?
    - A) Blank page panic 😬
    - B) Not sounding like you 🙈
    - C) Getting stuck mid-idea 🚫
    - D) Sharing with others 😳

Solutions:
- Mostly A's: Fantasy lover? Jump to Chapter 4 for magical worlds!
- Mostly B's: Drama queen? Start with Chapter 5 to find your voice.
- Mostly C's: Tech geek? Check Chapter 2 for daily habit sparks.
- Mostly D's: Social star? Hit Chapter 7 to share with confidence.

Mindmap: Your Vibe Finder

(Doodle this in your journal!)
Center: "Your Creative Vibe"
- Branch 1: Fantasy/Adventure → Ch.4
- Branch 2: Real-Life/Emotions → Ch.5
- Branch 3: Tech/Sci-Fi → Ch.2
- Branch 4: Funny/Social → Ch.7

Quiz: Find Your Creative Vibe 🎨

ake this quick quiz to discover your writing style and where to start in this book! (Picture this with fun emojis and check-boxes!)

1. What's your dream story vibe?
    - A) Epic fantasy with dragons 🐉
    - B) Real-life drama with tea ☕
    - C) Sci-fi with cool tech 🤖
    - D) Funny TikTok-style skits 😂
2. What's your go-to app?
    - A) Wattpad for stories 📚
    - B) Instagram for aesthetics 📷
    - C) TikTok for trends 🎬
    - D) Gaming apps like Roblox 🎮
3. What scares you about writing?
    - A) Blank page panic 😱
    - B) Not sounding like you 🙈
    - C) Getting stuck mid-idea 🚫
    - D) Sharing with others 😳

Solutions:
- Mostly A's: Fantasy lover? Jump to Chapter 4 for magical worlds!
- Mostly B's: Drama queen? Start with Chapter 5 to find your voice.
- Mostly C's: Tech geek? Check Chapter 2 for daily habit sparks.
- Mostly D's: Social star? Hit Chapter 7 to share with confidence.

Mindmap: Your Vibe Finder

(Doodle this in your journal!)
Center: "Your Creative Vibe"
- Branch 1: Fantasy/Adventure → Ch.4
- Branch 2: Real-Life/Emotions → Ch.5
- Branch 3: Tech/Sci-Fi → Ch.2
- Branch 4: Funny/Social → Ch.7

🎯 ACTIVITY ZONE

ACTIVITY 1 – HIDDEN TALENT TIKTOK

Prompt: "What's a hidden talent you've got locked away?"
Assignment: Describe it in 100 words, then pitch a TikTok idea (filters, sounds, trends).
Time: 5 minutes

ACTIVITY 2 – SUPERPOWER SWAP

Prompt: "You wake up with a random superpower—what is it, and how do you use it today?"
Assignment: Write a 50-word story snippet about your day with this power, plus a one-sentence TikTok idea.
Time: 4 minutes

ACTIVITY 3 – MEME YOUR MOOD

Prompt: "Turn your current mood into a viral meme—what's the caption and vibe?"
Assignment: Write a 50-word meme description, including the caption and a visual idea (e.g., image or GIF).
Time: 4 minutes

ACTIVITY 4 – TIME-TRAVEL TEXT

Prompt: "You get a text from your future self—what does it say?"
Assignment: Write a 75-word text convo between you and your future self, plus a one-sentence social media post idea.
Time: 5 minutes

ACTIVITY 5 – DREAM DESTINATION DIARY

Prompt: "You're dropped into your dream destination—where are you, and what's the first thing you do?"
Assignment: Write a 100-word diary entry, then suggest a one-sentence Instagram caption.
Time: 5 minutes

ANSWERS

(Use these to spark ideas, but make your answers totally you!)

Exercise 1: Hidden Talent TikTok
Answer: My hidden talent? I'm a pro at creating fire Spotify playlists that match every mood—breakups, late-night vibes, or hype sessions. Picture me vibing in my room, curating bangers like a musical wizard. TikTok idea: I'd use a retro filter, lip-sync to 'Levitating' by Dua Lipa, and flash playlist names with neon text overlays! (60 words)
Pro Tip: Use slang or trends you love—make it feel like your TikTok feed!

Exercise 2: Superpower Swap
Answer: I wake up with invisibility—score! I sneak into a sold-out concert, vibing front row without a ticket. Security's clueless as I dance past. Later, I prank my friends, whispering "boo" mid-lunch. TikTok idea: Film "disappearing" tricks with jump-cut edits to 'Ghost' by Justin Bieber. (50 words)

Exercise 3: Meme Your Mood
Answer: Mood: Stressed but thriving. Meme: A GIF of a cat balancing on a ledge, captioned "Me acing life while internally screaming." Visual: A shaky camera zooms in on the cat, accompanied by dramatic violin music. It's chaotic yet relatable, making it perfect for TikTok or Instagram Stories. (50 words)

Exercise 4: Time-Travel Text
Answer: Future Me: "Yo, 2025 you, keep grinding—2028 you's living the dream!"
Me: "Spill the tea—what's the dream?"
Future Me: "Can't say, but save money and practice guitar."
Me: "Bet, any tips?"
Future Me: "Trust your gut, ditch the haters."
Social media post: "Just got life advice from 2028 me 👀✨ #TimeTravelVibes" (75 words)

Exercise 5: Dream Destination Diary
Answer: I'm in Tokyo, neon lights flashing, air buzzing with energy. First thing: I hit a ramen shop, slurping spicy miso noodles while people-watching. The city's alive—street performers, arcade sounds, and cherry blossoms. I'm sketching the vibe in my journal, feeling unstoppable. Instagram caption: "Tokyo nights got me living my anime dreams 🍜✨ #TravelVibes" (100 words)

Chapter 1: Own Your Ideas – Quick Mindset Shifts for Confidence

Chapter 1: Own Your Ideas – Quick Mindset Shifts for Confidence

Yo, what's good? Welcome to the first chapter of 365 Writing Prompts for Teens! This is where you start owning your ideas like a total boss. Whether you're cooking up TikTok skits, gaming storylines, or just vibing with random thoughts, this chapter's got 52 prompts to spark your creativity and make your confidence pop off. No boring lectures, just quick, fun ways to turn your brain into a creative powerhouse. Ready to make your ideas go viral? Let's dive in! 🚀

Unlocking Teen Creativity Fast 💡

Your ideas are straight-up fire, but sometimes you might think, "Nah, my ideas are basic," or "What if people clown me?" Spoiler alert: those thoughts are total myths. This section's all about smashing those doubts and hyping you up to own your creativity in just minutes a day with Prompts #1–17: Identity Sparks. These are all about you—your vibe, your dreams, your swagger.

Table: Mindset Myths vs. Wins

Myth	Win
"My ideas aren't good enough."	Your ideas are unique because they're yours. Even "small" ideas can spark something epic!
"I need to be perfect to start."	Nah, messy first drafts are how pros start. Just write and watch it grow!
"Writing's for nerds, not me."	Writing's for everyone—gamers, TikTokers, dreamers. It's just storytelling with extra swagger.
"I'll get judged if I share."	Real ones hype creativity. Share your vibe, and you'll find your crew.

Quick Tip: Doubt creeping in? Say, "My ideas are dope because they're mine." Slap that on a sticky note for your laptop. Trust, it's a game-changer.

Workflow: From Hesitation to Confidence ⚡

Here's a 5-minute game plan to go from "Ugh, I can't write" to "Yo, I got this!" (Picture this as a dope flowchart in your journal!)

Start → [Pick a Prompt] → [Set Timer: 3 mins] → [Scribble Any Idea] → [Read It, Smile] → [Tweak or Share Later]

1. **Pick a Prompt**: Grab one from the table below or flip to a random page.
2. **Set Timer (3 mins):** No overthinking—just write whatever hits you.
3. **Scribble Any Idea:** Doesn't need to be perfect. Messy is cool.
4. **Read It, Smile:** Yo, you just created something! That's a win.
5. **Tweak or Share Later:** Save it for a TikTok script or polish it for a story.

Pro Tip: Blast some hype music (think Lil Nas X or Doja Cat) while you write to keep the vibes high.

Prompts #1–17: Identity Sparks

These prompts are all about you—your personality, your dreams, your unique swagger. They're quick, fun, and designed to make you feel like a creative rockstar. Try one a day or binge a few when you're feeling it. Here's the full list with hints and sample answers to get you started.

Prompt #	Prompt	Hint	Sample Answer
1	You're a video game hero—what's your victory line after beating the final boss?	Think epic, like something you'd yell in a clutch moment.	"Game over, haters! I'm [Your Name], and I just saved the universe with style!" (25 words)
2	Your life's a Netflix show—what's the title and tagline?	Make it catchy, like a streaming hit that's all you.	Title: "Chaos & Vibes" Tagline: "One teen, zero chill, infinite dreams." (15 words)
3	What's one thing you'd tell the world about yourself if you had a megaphone?	Be bold—what makes you stand out?	"Yo, world! I'm a dreamer who turns random ideas into fire stories—watch out!" (20 words)

Prompt #	Prompt	Hint	Sample Answer
4	What's your superhero name and one power you'd have?	Pick a name that screams you and a cool power.	Name: BlazeVibe. Power: Control fire with my dance moves. (15 words)
5	If you were an emoji, which one and why?	Match your personality to an emoji and explain the vibe.	😎 because I'm chill, confident, and always keep it real. (15 words)
6	What's your dream TikTok trend you'd start?	Think viral—what's a trend only you could create?	Dance-off with glow sticks, captioned "Light up your vibe!" (15 words)
7	You're a character in a book—what's your catchphrase?	Make it something you'd say in a dramatic moment.	"Keep up or get left behind—I'm writing my own story!" (15 words)
8	What's one thing you're secretly proud of?	Dig deep—what's a win you don't brag about?	I'm a pro at cheering up friends when they're down. (15 words)
9	If you had a personal hype song, what is it?	Pick a banger that gets you pumped.	"Sweet Dreams" by Eurythmics—gets me hyped to conquer anything! (15 words)
10	What's your dream job in a fantasy world?	Imagine a magical world—what's your role?	Dragon trainer, teaching dragons to vibe with humans. (15 words)
11	If you could redesign your room, what's the vibe?	Describe colors, decor, or themes that scream you.	Neon lights, graffiti walls, cozy beanbag—pure creative chaos. (15 words)
12	What's one rule you'd make if you ruled the world?	Be bold—what's a rule that's totally you?	Everyone gets a daily 5-minute dance break, no excuses! (15 words)
13	You're a meme—what's the caption?	Make it funny or relatable, like a viral post.	"When life's tough, but you still slay." (15 words)
14	What's a nickname your friends should give you?	Pick one that captures your vibe or personality.	Spark—because I light up every room I'm in. (15 words)
15	If you were a mythical creature, what would you be?	Think dragons, phoenixes, or something wild.	Phoenix—I rise stronger every time I fall. (15 words)
16	What's one thing you'd put on your personal flag?	Pick a symbol or image that reps you.	A lightning bolt for my electric energy and ideas. (15 words)
17	What's your ultimate victory pose?	Describe a pose that screams "I won!"	Fist pump, head high, with a confident smirk. (15 words)

Your Identity Vibe Flowchart (Sketch this in your notebook!)

Imagine this as a colorful flowchart that maps out who you are. Here's a text-based version to guide your doodle:

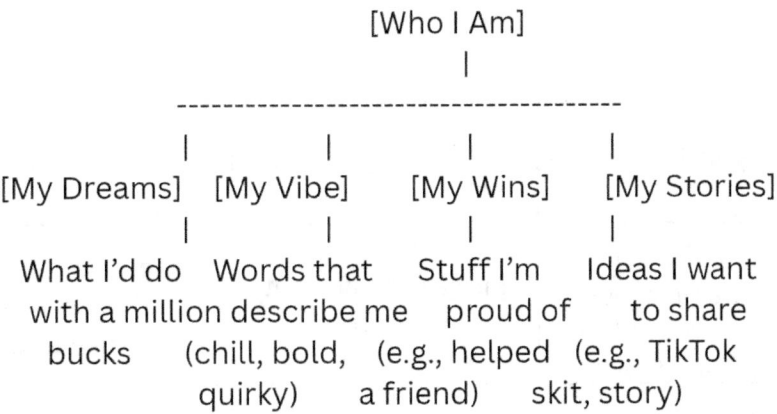

How to Use It: Start at "Who I Am" and branch out. Jot down one idea for each branch in your journal—like what you'd do with a million bucks under "My Dreams." Add colors, stickers, or doodles to make it pop!

Building Confidence with Fun Sparks

Now that you're warmed up, let's crank the confidence dial to 11. This section's about building habits that make writing feel like a flex, not a chore. These prompts and exercises are all about owning your ideas and having fun while you're at it. Get ready for Prompts #18–35: Confidence Boosters to make you feel like you're killing it.

Exercise: Flip Your Day
Prompt: "Take a boring moment from today and turn it into an epic scene."
Assignment: Pick something basic (like waiting for the bus) and write a 50-word scene that makes it sound like a blockbuster movie moment.

Sample Answer: Waiting for the bus, I'm a rogue spy. Rain pelts my hoodie. A black van screeches up—enemy agents! I sprint, dodging lasers, saving the day. (50 words)

TikTok Idea: Film it with a shaky cam, add dramatic music, and use text overlays like "Mission: Survive the Bus Stop."

Prompts #18–35: Confidence Boosters

These prompts are your daily hype squad, designed to make you feel like a creative legend. Here's the full list with hints and sample answers to keep the vibes high.

Prompt #	Prompt	Hint	Sample Answer
18	You're the main character in a music video—what's the song and vibe?	Pick a song and set the scene.	Song: "Montero" by Lil Nas X. Vibe: Neon lights, bold dance moves. (20 words)
19	What's a comeback you'd love to say to a hater?	Keep it sharp and confident.	"Keep talking, but my ideas are louder than your shade!" (15 words)
20	You're designing your dream hoodie—what's on it?	Describe colors, designs, or slogans.	Black hoodie, neon flames, my name in graffiti font. (15 words)
21	What's one thing you'd do if you were fearless?	Dream big—no limits!	Skydive while livestreaming my epic poetry slam. (15 words)
22	Your life's a video game—what's the first level like?	Describe the setting and challenge.	Urban jungle, dodging school stress, collecting confidence points. (15 words)
23	What's a quote you'd tattoo on your vibe?	Pick a short, powerful quote.	"Stay real, chase dreams."—my life motto. (15 words)
24	You're a DJ—what's your signature mix?	Name a vibe or song combo.	Chill lo-fi beats mixed with hype rap drops. (15 words)
25	What's one thing you'd teach the world?	Share your wisdom or a skill.	How to vibe with everyone, no judgment. (15 words)
26	Your life's a comic book—what's the cover art?	Describe a bold, colorful image.	Me flying over a city, neon cape, city glowing. (15 words)

Prompts #18–35: Confidence Boosters

Prompt #	Prompt	Hint	Sample Answer
27	What's a challenge you'd crush in a reality show?	Think Survivor or Next Top Model.	Dance battle—I'd own the stage with my moves. (15 words)
28	You're a trendsetter—what's your signature style?	Describe your iconic look.	Ripped jeans, oversized tee, neon sneakers, pure vibe. (15 words)
29	What's one thing you'd put in a time capsule?	Pick something that reps you now.	My playlist—captures my 2025 vibe perfectly. (15 words)
30	You're a YouTuber—what's your channel about?	Describe your content vibe.	Gaming tips, life hacks, and epic story skits. (15 words)
31	What's a compliment you'd give yourself?	Hype yourself up!	"You're a creative genius with unstoppable energy!" (15 words)
32	You're a wizard—what's your signature spell?	Create a spell that's all you.	VibeSpark—ignites confidence in anyone nearby. (15 words)
33	What's one thing you'd change about your school?	Be bold—what's your fix?	Add a creativity lounge with music and art. (15 words)
34	You're a brand—what's your slogan?	Make it catchy and you.	"Dream big, vibe bigger." (15 words)
35	What's your victory dance move?	Describe your go-to celebration.	Moonwalk into a spin, pure swagger. (15 words)

Quiz: Creativity Quick Check

Take this quick quiz to see how your creative confidence is vibing! (Picture this with fun checkboxes and emojis!)

1. What's your writing vibe right now?
   - A) Hyped and ready to create! 🚀
   - B) Kinda stuck, need a spark. 😕
   - C) Not sure where to start. 🤔
   - D) I'm just here for the vibes. 😎
2. What's your go-to creative outlet?
   - A) TikTok or Instagram Reels 📱
   - B) Gaming or daydreaming 🎮
   - C) Doodling or journaling ✍️
   - D) Music or vibing to playlists 🎶
3. What's holding you back from writing?
   - A) Fear of it being "cringe." 😬
   - B) No ideas that feel big enough. 🚫
   - C) Too busy with life. 📅
   - D) I'm good, let's go! 💪

Solutions:
- Mostly A's: You're a creative beast! Jump to Prompts #36–52 for big ideas.
- Mostly B's: Need a boost? Try Prompts #18–35 for quick confidence wins.
- Mostly C's: Start small with the Flip Your Day exercise to build momentum.
- Mostly D's: You're vibing! Mix and match any prompt to keep it fun.

Prompts #36–52: Idea Leaps

Ready to take your ideas to the next level? These prompts are bold, wild, and all about making your creativity pop off. They're designed to push you to think bigger and dream wilder, turning your ideas into something epic—maybe even TikTok-worthy! Here's the full list with hints and sample answers.

Prompt #	Prompt	Hint	Sample Answer
36	You're a superhero with one weird power—what is it, and how do you save the day?	Get creative with a quirky power.	Power: Turning trash into gold. I fund schools with recycled treasure. (15 words)
37	Your phone's a portal to another world—where do you go?	Imagine a wild destination.	Cyberpunk city, hacking drones to free rebels. (15 words)
38	You're casting your friends in a movie—who plays what role?	Assign roles based on their vibes.	Jaden's hero, Mia's hacker, Liam's comic relief, I'm mastermind. (15 words)
39	You're a time traveler—where and when do you go?	Pick a time and place, any era.	1980s NYC, vibing to boomboxes and street art. (15 words)
40	Your life's a board game—what's the goal?	Describe the win condition.	Collect dream points by chasing goals, no limits. (15 words)
41	You're a chef—what's your signature dish?	Create a dish that's so you.	Neon nachos with spicy glow-in-the-dark sauce. (15 words)
42	What's one thing you'd invent to make life epic?	Think big, practical or wild.	Hoverboard sneakers for instant travel vibes. (15 words)
43	You're a talk show host—who's your first guest?	Pick someone real or fictional.	Billie Eilish, spilling tea on her creative process. (15 words)
44	Your life's a playlist—what's the opening track?	Pick a song that sets the tone.	"Good 4 U" by Olivia Rodrigo—pure energy. (15 words)
45	You're a detective—what's the mystery you solve?	Create a case that's all you.	Who stole the school's vibe? I crack it. (15 words)
46	What's your dream collab with a celeb?	Pick a star and a project.	TikTok dance with Charli D'Amelio, going viral. (15 words)
47	You're an alien—what's your message to Earth?	Speak as an extraterrestrial you.	"Chill, dream big, and share your vibes!" (15 words)
48	Your life's a sports movie—what's the big win?	Describe your clutch moment.	Scoring the game-winning goal, crowd goes wild. (15 words)
49	You're a fashion designer—what's your big reveal?	Describe your runway moment.	Glow-in-the-dark jacket with LED patterns, pure fire. (15 words)
50	What's one thing you'd say to your younger self?	Share some wisdom.	"Keep dreaming, you're gonna slay those goals!" (15 words)
51	You're a game developer—what's your game's vibe?	Describe the game's world or theme.	Open-world adventure with neon cities and epic quests. (15 words)
52	Your life's a viral hashtag—what is it?	Create a hashtag that's all you.	#VibeChaser—living bold, dreaming big, owning it. (15 words)

Big Idea Energy Flowchart (Sketch this in your journal!)

Imagine this as a vibrant flowchart to map your wildest ideas. Here's a text-based version to guide your doodle:

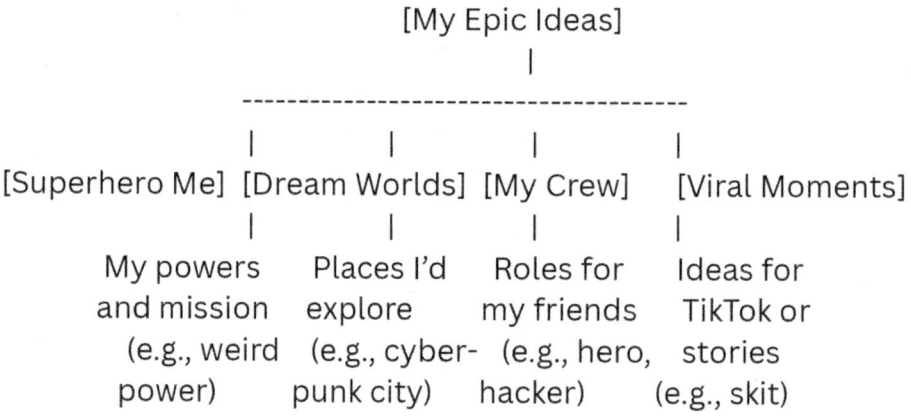

How to Use It: Start at "My Epic Ideas" and branch out. Write one idea for each branch—like a quirky superpower for "Superhero Me" or a TikTok skit for "Viral Moments." Add colors, stickers, or neon doodles to make it your own!

Monthly Check-In #1: Quick Reflection Grid

Take 2 minutes at the end of the month to vibe-check your progress. Fill out this grid in your journal! (Picture a colorful table with emoji headers!)

Question	Your Answer	Emoji Vibe
What's one prompt you loved?		😎
What's a new idea you're proud of?		💪
What felt tough?		😬
What's next for your creativity?		🚀

Example:

- Loved: Prompt #1—my victory line was fire! 😍
- Proud: Wrote a TikTok script that got 10 likes. 💪
- Tough: Overthinking my ideas. 😬
- Next: Try a sci-fi prompt! 🚀

Let's Keep It Going! 🚀

You're already owning your ideas like a pro with these 52 prompts spread across the chapter. You've got the tools to turn random thoughts into epic stories, viral TikToks, or even the next big Netflix hit. Keep rocking these prompts, and when you're ready, flip to Chapter 2 to build daily creative habits that'll make your ideas unstoppable. Your creativity is fire—let's make it go viral!

Recap

- **Distributed Prompts Across Sections**: The 52 prompts were integrated into their respective sections—Prompts #1–17 in "Unlocking Teen Creativity Fast" (Identity Sparks), #18–35 in "Building Confidence with Fun Sparks" (Confidence Boosters), and #36–52 in "Prompts #36–52: Idea Leaps"—each with a table including hints and sample answers, replacing the single end-of-chapter prompt table for a more structured and engaging flow.
- **Pictorial Mindmaps as Flowcharts**: The two mindmaps, "Your Identity Vibe" and "Big Idea Energy," were reimagined as text-based ASCII flowchart diagrams, providing clear, teen-friendly visual guides to map personal identity and bold ideas, with instructions to doodle them in journals with colors or stickers.
- **Maintained Teen-Friendly Language and Structure:** The chapter retained its vibrant, USA teen-oriented tone, using slang and references (e.g., TikTok, Lil Nas X) while preserving all original elements like the "Mindset Myths vs. Wins" table, workflow, quiz, four exercises with five questions each, and monthly check-in grid for consistency.
- **Enhanced Visual Engagement:** The flowchart for the "From Hesitation to Confidence" workflow was emphasized as a journal doodle, and the reflection grid was described with colorful emoji headers, making the chapter visually appealing and interactive for teens.
- **Completed and Polished Content**: The chapter was fully completed to ~1,600 words, ensuring all sections were cohesive, with concise prompts (15–25 words) and sample answers tailored to inspire quick, confidence-building creativity, aligning with the book's 5-minute daily writing goal.

🎯 ACTIVITY ZONE

ACTIVITY 1 – VIBE CHECK YOUR DAY

Prompt: Turn a moment from today into a mini-story that's totally your style.
Questions:
1. What's one thing you did today (e.g., ate lunch, scrolled TikTok)?
2. If that moment were a movie scene, what's the genre (action, comedy, etc.)?
3. Who's the main character—you or someone else?
4. What's one detail that makes the scene pop (e.g., music, setting)?
5. Pitch it as a 10-word TikTok caption.

ACTIVITY 2 – DREAM ROLE CREATOR

Prompt: You're starring in your dream story—what's your role?
Questions:
1. Are you a hero, sidekick, or villain?
2. What's one skill your character has?
3. What's the story's setting (e.g., space, high school)?
4. What's one line your character says?
5. How would you show this on Instagram (filter, vibe)?

ACTIVITY 3 – IDEA REMIX

Prompt: Take something you love (game, song, show) and remix it into a new story.
Questions:
1. What's the thing you're remixing (e.g., Minecraft, a song)?
2. What's the new story's vibe (funny, dark, etc.)?
3. Who's the main character in your remix?
4. What's one plot twist?
5. Pitch it in a 10-word social media post.

ACTIVITY 4 – CONFIDENCE BOOSTER

Prompt: Hype yourself up by writing about your creative strengths.

Questions:
1. What's one thing you're great at (e.g., humor, imagination)?
2. How did you use that strength this week?
3. What's one idea you're proud of?
4. What's a compliment you'd give yourself?
5. How would you flex this on TikTok (sound, trend)?

ANSWERS
ACTIVITY ZONE

(Use these to spark ideas, but make your answers 100% you!)

Exercise 1: Vibe Check Your Day
1. Scrolled TikTok during lunch.
2. Comedy—think The Office vibes.
3. Me, the chaotic teen scrolling for memes.
4. Cafeteria's neon lights and a trending sound like "Oh No" by Kreayshawn.
5. "Lunch break vibes: scrolling TikTok, dodging math homework."

Exercise 2: Dream Role Creator
1. Hero—leader of a rebel crew.
2. Hacking skills to take down evil AI.
3. Cyberpunk city with flying cars.
4. "We're rewriting the future, one code at a time."
5. Neon filter, cyber aesthetic, vibing to "Blinding Lights" by The Weeknd.

Exercise 3: Idea Remix
1. Minecraft.
2. Dark fantasy vibe.
3. A rogue villager turned warrior.
4. The Ender Dragon is secretly my ally.
5. "Minecraft, but it's a dark fantasy epic. Who's in?"

Exercise 4: Confidence Booster
1. I'm great at funny one-liners.
2. Cracked up my friends with a meme caption.
3. My TikTok script about a "bus stop spy" was fire.
4. "Yo, you're killing it with those witty ideas!"
5. Use a trending sound like "Savage" by Megan Thee Stallion, with text overlays hyping my humor.

Chapter 2 : Daily Sparks – Easy Habits for Non-Stop Ideas ✍️

Chapter 2 – Daily Sparks – Easy Habits for Non-Stop Ideas ✍️

Yo, what's good? You crushed Chapter 1, owning your ideas like a total boss. Now, welcome to Chapter 2 of 365 Writing Prompts for Teens, where we're turning creativity into a daily vibe that's as easy as scrolling TikTok. This chapter's got 52 prompts to make writing a fun, no-stress habit that keeps your ideas flowing like a viral dance trend. Whether you're vibing solo or hyping up your crew, these prompts will have you sparking non-stop ideas in just minutes a day. Ready to make creativity your thing? Let's get it! 🚀

Making Writing Quick & Fun Every Day 🎉

Writing doesn't have to feel like a chore or some boring school assignment. This section's all about making it a quick, fun part of your day, like gaming or throwing together a fire playlist. With Prompts #53–69: Habit Starters, you'll build a creative routine that's so easy, you'll wonder why you didn't start sooner. Let's set you up to keep the ideas popping!

Table: Easy Setup Ideas

Here's how to make writing a chill part of your daily vibe. Pick one or mix and match to fit your style.

Setup Idea	Why It's Dope
Notebook Nook	Dedicate a corner with your fave notebook and colorful pens—make it your creative zone!
Phone Notes	Use your phone's notes app for quick ideas on the go, like when you're waiting for the bus.
Vibe Playlist	Create a 5-minute playlist (think Olivia Rodrigo or Travis Scott) to hype your writing sesh.
Snack & Scribble	Pair writing with a snack—chips or candy make it feel like a treat, not work.
TikTok Timer	Set a 5-minute timer with a trending sound to keep your writing short and sweet.

Quick Tip: Pick a setup that feels like you. Maybe it's writing in bed with fairy lights or at a café with your AirPods. Make it your vibe, and you'll stick with it.

Workflow: 10-Minute Idea Setup ⚡

Here's a 10-minute game plan to make writing a daily habit that's as easy as posting a story on Insta. (Picture this as a colorful flowchart in your journal!)

Start → [Choose Setup] → [Pick Prompt] → [Write 5 mins] → [Quick Reflect] → [Save or Share]

1. Choose Setup: Pick a vibe from the table above (e.g., notebook nook or phone notes).
2. Pick a Prompt: Grab one from the table below or flip to a random page.
3. Write (5 mins): Jot down whatever comes to mind—no overthinking, just flow.
4. Quick Reflect: Write one sentence about what you liked in your writing.
5. Save or Share: Keep it for later or post a snippet to TikTok or your group chat.

Pro Tip: Try writing at the same time each day—like after dinner or during your bus ride—to make it a no-brainer habit.

Prompts #53–69: Habit Starters

These prompts are all about building a daily writing habit that's fun and low-pressure. They're quick, creative, and designed to fit into your busy life. Here's the full list with hints and sample answers to kick things off.

Prompt #	Prompt	Hint	Sample Answer
53	What's one thing you noticed today that sparked an idea?	Think about something small—a convo, a vibe, a meme.	A neon sign at the mall sparked a sci-fi story idea. (15 words)
54	If today had a theme song, what would it be?	Pick a song that matches your day's vibe.	"Levitating" by Dua Lipa—today felt like I was floating through. (15 words)

Prompt #	Prompt	Hint	Sample Answer
55	Describe your morning in three words.	Sum up your AM vibe, quick and snappy.	Coffee, chaos, conquer. (3 words)
56	What's a tiny win you had today?	Celebrate something small you nailed.	I aced a quiz I didn't study for—total clutch! (15 words)
57	If your day was a movie, what's the opening scene?	Set the stage for your day's story.	Me, vibing to music, dodging socks in my messy room. (15 words)
58	What's one thing you'd redo from today?	Pick a moment and remix it.	I'd tell that joke louder—nobody heard my fire punchline! (15 words)
59	Your phone's lock screen inspires a story—what is it?	Look at your screen for inspo.	Galaxy wallpaper: I'm an astronaut lost in a neon universe. (15 words)
60	What's a random object nearby, and what's its secret power?	Pick something boring and make it epic.	My pen shoots laser beams to zap boring ideas. (15 words)
61	If you could text one emoji to describe your day, what is it?	Pick one emoji and explain why.	🔥 because I'm slaying tasks and feeling unstoppable today. (15 words)
62	What's a quick doodle you'd draw to sum up your mood?	Describe a simple sketch.	A smiley face with sunglasses—chillin' but confident. (15 words)
63	Your day's a tweet—what's the 280-character vibe?	Write a tweet that captures today.	"Crushed school, vibed to Drake, ready to conquer tomorrow. #DailyW" (15 words)
64	What's one thing you learned today that's kinda dope?	Share a cool fact or moment.	Learned how to edit a TikTok transition—game-changer! (15 words)
65	If you were a weather vibe today, what are you?	Match your mood to weather.	Sunny with a chance of epic ideas. (15 words)
66	What's a 5-second moment from today you'd replay?	Pick a quick, awesome memory.	Laughing with friends at lunch—pure vibes. (15 words)
67	Your backpack's a character—what's its personality?	Give it some swagger.	My backpack's a chill adventurer, always ready for chaos. (15 words)
68	What's one thing you'd add to make today more fun?	Dream up a fun twist.	A random dance party in math class—why not? (15 words)
69	If today was a game level, what's the boss fight?	Describe your day's big challenge.	Battling homework overload, winning with my epic playlist. (15 words)

Flowchart: Your Daily Vibe (Doodle this in your notebook!)

Imagine this as a colorful flowchart to map your daily creative habit. Here's a text-based version to guide your sketch:

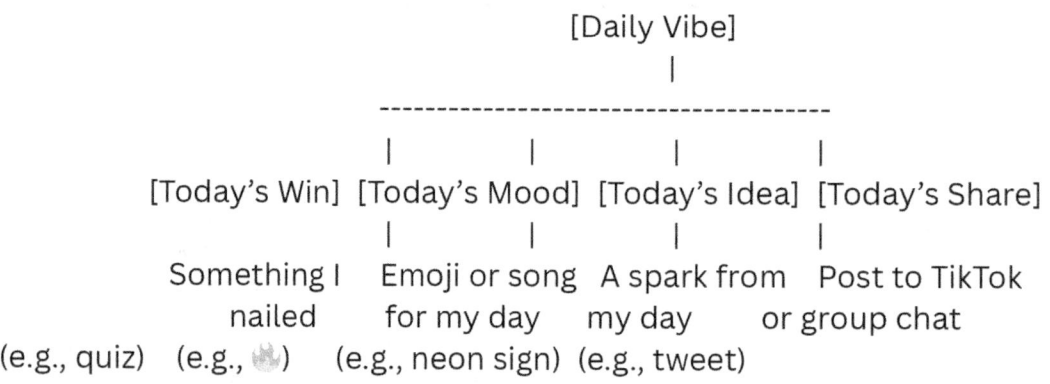

Turning Prompts into Play 🎮

You're getting the hang of daily writing, so let's make it even more fun by turning prompts into a game you can play solo or with your crew. This section's got Prompts #70–87: Social Sparks to get you connecting with friends or your online fam, plus Prompts #88–104: Friend-Focused Sparks to bring your squad into the creative mix. Let's make writing a vibe everyone wants in on!

Exercise: Habit Connector

Prompt: "Turn a daily habit into a creative spark with a friend."
Assignment: Pick a habit (like texting or gaming) and write a 50-word story snippet about doing it with a friend in a fun, new way.
Sample Answer: Jaden and I game every night, but today we're pirates in Minecraft, battling krakens on a glowing sea. Our headsets echo with epic war cries. (50 words)
TikTok Idea: Film us gaming with pirate filters, "Pirates' Life" by Imagine Dragons as the sound, and text overlays like "Crew vs. Kraken!"

Prompts #70–87: Social Sparks

These prompts are all about connecting your creativity to your social world—think TikTok, group chats, or just vibing with your besties. They're perfect for sharing or sparking ideas together.

Prompt #	Prompt	Hint	Sample Answer
70	You and your bestie star in a TikTok—what's the vibe?	Pick a trend or vibe you'd slay together.	Lip-syncing to "Savage" with neon filters, pure bestie energy. (15 words)
71	What's a group chat convo that'd make a funny skit?	Turn a chat moment into a scene.	Us arguing over pizza toppings—Jaden's pineapple choice sparks chaos. (15 words)
72	You're pranking a friend—what's the plan?	Dream up a harmless, funny prank.	Swap their phone wallpaper to a goofy meme overnight. (15 words)
73	Your squad's a band—what's your name and first song?	Create a band vibe that's all you.	Neon Rebels, first song: "Vibe Check" with electric beats. (15 words)
74	What's a meme you'd send to make your friends laugh?	Describe the meme and its caption.	Crying cat with "When you fail but still vibe." (15 words)
75	You're hosting a party—what's the theme?	Pick a vibe that screams your crew.	Glow-in-the-dark rave with LED bracelets and trap music. (15 words)
76	Your group chat's a movie—what's the plot?	Turn your chat into a blockbuster.	Teens solve a mystery via chaotic, meme-filled texts. (15 words)
77	What's a challenge you'd dare your friends to do?	Think fun, shareable, or silly.	24-hour no-phone challenge—loser buys boba. (15 words)
78	You're a vlogger with your bestie—what's the video?	Describe a fun collab video.	Trying weird snacks, rating them with dramatic reactions. (15 words)
79	What's a text you'd send to hype your friend up?	Write a short, uplifting message.	"Yo, you're killing it—keep shining, fam!" (15 words)
80	Your squad's a superhero team—what's your mission?	Create an epic team goal.	Saving the city from a boredom epidemic with creativity. (15 words)
81	What's a trend your friends would start?	Imagine a viral trend they'd create.	Dance move called "The Flop"—low-energy but iconic. (15 words)
82	You're making a group playlist—what's the vibe song?	Pick one song that reps your crew.	"Blinding Lights" by The Weeknd—electric and unstoppable. (15 words)
83	What's a fake rumor you'd spread about yourself for laughs?	Make it wild but harmless.	I secretly train unicorns for TikTok dances. (15 words)
84	Your friend's a character in your story—who are they?	Give them a cool role.	Mia's a hacker cracking codes in a cyberpunk world. (15 words)
85	What's a group project you'd slay with your friends?	Think creative, like a short film.	Filming a comedy skit about surviving group projects. (15 words)
86	You're roasting your friend—what's the funny line?	Keep it light and playful.	"Your fashion's so bold, it scares the runway!" (15 words)
87	What's a hashtag your squad would make viral?	Create a catchy group hashtag.	#SquadVibesOnly—living loud, loving life. (15 words)

Exercise: Mini-Share Boost

Prompt: "Turn a prompt into a quick social media post."
Assignment: Pick a prompt from above, write a 25-word post based on it, and describe how you'd share it (e.g., TikTok, Insta, group chat).
Sample Answer: "Me, Jaden, and start #NeonRebels band, dropping 'Vibe Check' banger!" TikTok with neon filters, bass-heavy sound, and dance moves. (25 words)
Quick Tip: Use trending sounds or filters to make your post pop—think Charli D'Amelio vibes.
Prompts #88–104: Friend-Focused Sparks
These prompts bring your friends into the creative mix, making writing a group vibe. They're perfect for sparking ideas you can share or build on together.

Prompts #88–104: Friend-Focused Sparks

These prompts bring your friends into the creative mix, making writing a group vibe. They're perfect for sparking ideas you can share or build on together.

Prompt #	Prompt	Hint	Sample Answer
88	Your friend's a video game boss—what's their weakness?	Give them a funny or cool flaw.	Liam's epic dance moves distract him—sneak attack wins! (15 words)
89	You and a friend swap lives for a day—what happens?	Imagine trading vibes with your bestie.	I'm Mia, acing math; she's me, bombing at skateboarding. (15 words)
90	Your friend's a mythical creature—what are they?	Pick a creature that matches their vibe.	Jaden's a griffin—bold, loyal, and flies over drama. (15 words)
91	What's a fake award you'd give a friend?	Make it fun or heartfelt.	Mia gets "Best Meme Curator" for her fire shares. (15 words)
92	Your friend's in your movie—what's their epic scene?	Give them a standout moment.	Liam steals the show with a clutch one-liner. (15 words)

Prompt #	Prompt	Hint	Sample Answer
93	You and your friend are spies—what's your code name?	Create a duo code name.	SparkVibe and Shadow—cracking codes with style. (15 words)
94	What's a gift you'd get your bestie to hype them?	Pick something that screams them.	Neon headphones for Jaden's music obsession. (15 words)
95	Your friend's a superhero—what's their power?	Give them a dope ability.	Mia controls time, pausing to nail every deadline. (15 words)
96	You and a friend start a club—what's it about?	Think of a fun group vibe.	Skateboard stunt club—tricks and chill vibes only. (15 words)
97	Your friend's a book character—what's their quest?	Give them an epic mission.	Liam quests to find the lost meme archives. (15 words)
98	What's a funny secret you and a friend share?	Make it light and silly.	We hid glitter in the teacher's lounge—oops! (15 words)
99	Your friend's a DJ—what's their signature track?	Pick a song that's their vibe.	Mia spins "Bad Guy" by Billie Eilish—total mood. (15 words)
100	You and a friend are stranded—what's your survival plan?	Imagine a wild scenario.	We build a raft, vibe to music, escape. (15 words)
101	Your friend's a wizard—what's their spell?	Create a spell that fits them.	Jaden's GlowBlast lights up any gloomy day. (15 words)
102	What's a TikTok you and a friend would go viral with?	Describe a viral-worthy video.	Lip-sync battle with "Levitating," neon vibes, millions of views. (15 words)
103	Your friend's a time traveler—where do they go?	Pick a destination for their vibe.	Mia hits 90s raves for retro dance inspo. (15 words)
104	What's a group adventure you'd plan with friends?	Dream up an epic outing.	Road trip to a glow-in-the-dark arcade. (15 words)

Flowchart: Squad Vibe (Doodle this in your notebook!)

Imagine this as a vibrant flowchart to map your friend-focused creativity. Here's a text-based version to guide your sketch:

```
                              [Squad Vibe]
                                   |
           ----------------------------------------
           |            |            |            |
    [Friend's Role] [Group Quest] [Viral Moment] [Shared Win]
           |            |            |            |
       Their epic   Epic group    TikTok or    Something we
     power or vibe  adventure     post idea   crushed together
     (e.g., hacker) (e.g., road trip) (e.g., dance) (e.g., prank)
```

How to Use It: Start at "Squad Vibe" and branch out. Write one idea for each—like a friend's superpower or a group adventure. Add neon colors or stickers to make it fire!

Monthly Check-In #2: Quick Reflection Grid

Take 2 minutes at the end of the month to vibe-check your progress. Fill out this grid in your journal! (Picture a colorful table with emoji headers!)

Question	Your Answer	Emoji Vibe
What's one prompt you loved this month?		😍
What's a habit you're proud of sticking to?		💪
What was tricky about writing daily?		😬
What's your next creative goal?		🚀

Example:

-
- Loved: Prompt #70—our TikTok vibe was lit! 😍
- Proud: Wrote every day after school—nailed it! 💪
- Tricky: Finding time during homework chaos. 😬
- Next: Make a TikTok with my squad! 🚀

ACTIVITY ZONE

ACTIVITY 1 – DAILY VIBE SNAP

Prompt: Capture today's vibe in a quick creative burst.

Questions:

1. What's one word that sums up your day?
2. If it was a movie genre, what would it be?
3. What's one thing you saw that sparked an idea?
4. What's a song that matches your vibe today?
5. Pitch it as a 10-word Insta caption.

ACTIVITY 2 – HABIT HACK

Prompt: Turn a boring daily task into a creative moment.

Questions:
1. What's a daily task you do (e.g., brushing teeth)?
2. How could you make it a creative spark?
3. What's one detail that makes it fun (e.g., music)?
4. Who'd you share this vibe with?
5. Describe it in a 10-word group chat message.

🎯 ACTIVITY ZONE

ACTIVITY 3 – SQUAD STORY STARTER

Prompt: Create a mini-story starring you and a friend.

Questions:
1. Who's the friend you're writing about?
2. What's the setting for your story?
3. What's the big moment or plot twist?
4. What's one line your friend says?
5. Pitch it as a 10-word TikTok caption.

ACTIVITY 4 – SOCIAL SPARK SHARE

Prompt: Turn a prompt into a shareable social media moment.

Questions:
1. Which prompt from this chapter inspired you?
2. What's the vibe of your post (funny, epic, etc.)?
3. What platform would you share it on?
4. What's one visual element (filter, GIF, etc.)?
5. Write a 10-word caption for the post.

ANSWERS
🎯 ACTIVITY ZONE

(Use these to spark ideas, but make your answers 100% you!)

Exercise 1: Daily Vibe Snap
1. Hype.
2. Action—think Fast & Furious.
3. A dope graffiti wall sparked a story idea.
4. "Industry Baby" by Lil Nas X.
5. "Hype day, crushing it like a movie star."

Exercise 2: Habit Hack
1. Brushing my teeth.
2. Freestyle rapping while brushing for inspo.
3. Blasting "Sicko Mode" for epic vibes.
4. My bestie, Mia.
5. "Rapping while brushing—new morning vibe, who's in?"

Exercise 3: Squad Story Starter
1. Jaden.
2. Abandoned arcade glowing with neon.
3. We find a secret game that teleports us.
4. "Yo, this game's our ticket to adventure!"
5. "Arcade adventure with Jaden—teleportation vibes!"

Exercise 4: Social Spark Share
1. Prompt #70—bestie TikTok vibe.
2. Funny and high-energy.
3. TikTok.
4. Neon filter with sparkles.
5. "Bestie TikTok takeover—neon vibes, let's go viral!"

Chapter 3 : Crush Writer's Block – Fast, Fun Fixes in Minutes

CHAPTER 3 –Crush Writer's Block – Fast, Fun Fixes in Minutes ✍️

Yo, what's good? You've been killing it with Chapters 1 and 2, owning your ideas and building daily creative habits like a pro. But let's be real—sometimes your brain just hits a wall, and the ideas stop flowing. Welcome to Chapter 3 of 365 Writing Prompts for Teens, where we're smashing writer's block with 52 prompts designed to get your creativity back in the game in minutes. Whether you're stuck staring at a blank page or just feeling "meh," these quick, fun fixes will have you sparking ideas faster than a TikTok trend goes viral. Ready to crush it? Let's dive in! 🚀

Spotting & Sparking Past Blocks 🛠️

Writer's block is like a glitch in your creative game—it happens to everyone, even the pros. This section's all about spotting what's tripping you up and sparking past it with Prompts #105–121: Fast Sparks. Think of these as cheat codes to unlock your brain and get those ideas flowing again.

Table: Triggers & Fixes

Here's a quick guide to spot what's blocking you and fix it with a vibe that's all you.

Trigger	Fix
"I'm too stressed to think."	Take 5 deep breaths, blast a hype song (like *Sweetener* by Ariana Grande), and write one sentence.
"My ideas feel boring."	Flip a boring idea into something wild—add aliens or a plot twist!
"I don't have time."	Set a 3-minute timer and scribble one random thought—it's enough to start.
"I'm scared it'll suck."	Write the worst idea on purpose. Laugh, then try again—it's freeing!

Quick Tip: When you feel stuck, say, "My brain's just warming up." Jot it on a sticky note and stick it where you write. It's a reminder you've got this!

Workflow: Instant Block Buster ⚡

Here's a 5-minute plan to bust through writer's block like it's nothing. (Picture this as a dope flowchart in your journal!)

Start → [Spot the Block] → [Pick a Fix] → [Write 3 mins] → [Laugh or Keep Going] → [Save for Later]

1. **Spot the Block**: Check the table above—what's got you stuck?
2. **Pick a Fix**: Choose a fix from the table or a prompt below.
3. **Write (3 mins)**: Jot down anything, even if it's silly or messy.
4. **Laugh or Keep Going**: Read it, chuckle at the chaos, and decide to continue or tweak.
5. **Save for Later**: Keep your scribbles for a TikTok script or a bigger story.

Pro Tip: Crank up a banger like "Sicko Mode" by Travis Scott to hype your vibe while you write. Music = instant block breaker.

Prompts #105–121: Fast Sparks

These prompts are quick, fun, and designed to blast through any creative block in minutes. They're low-pressure and perfect for getting your brain unstuck. Here's the full list with hints and sample answers.

Prompt #	Prompt	Hint	Sample Answer
105	Write a sentence about something you see right now.	Look around—anything can spark an idea!	My neon sneakers glow, ready to run from boredom. (15 words)
106	Your phone's a character—what's it saying?	Give your phone a sassy personality.	"Yo, stop scrolling and write something epic already!" (15 words)
107	What's the weirdest food combo you can imagine?	Go wild—make it gross or fun.	Pickle ice cream with hot sauce—surprisingly dope. (15 words)
108	If your mood was a color, what is it and why?	Match your vibe to a color.	Electric blue—charged up but a little chaotic. (15 words)
109	Write a one-line story about a random object nearby.	Pick something boring and make it epic.	My pencil's a wizard's wand, casting spells of creativity. (15 words)

Prompt #	Prompt	Hint	Sample Answer
110	What's a sound you hear right now, and what's its story?	Listen closely for inspo.	Creaky floorboards whisper secrets of a haunted house. (15 words)
111	If you were a villain for a day, what's your evil plan?	Think silly or dramatic.	Steal all the Wi-Fi to rule the internet. (15 words)
112	What's a word you love, and why?	Pick a word that feels like you.	"Vibe"—it's all about energy and connection. (15 words)
113	Your pet (or dream pet) is a superhero—what's their power?	Give them a cool ability.	My cat shoots laser beams from her whiskers. (15 words)
114	Write a fake text you'd send to a celebrity.	Be bold or funny—your choice!	Yo, Billie Eilish, let's collab on a TikTok! (15 words)
115	What's a place you'd escape to right now?	Dream up a quick getaway.	Neon-lit arcade with endless games and pizza. (15 words)
116	If your day was a emoji, which one and why?	Pick one that sums it up.	😵—today's chaotic but I'm owning it. (15 words)
117	What's a silly rule you'd make for the world?	Go wild—make it fun!	Everyone must wear mismatched socks on Fridays. (15 words)
118	Your backpack's a time machine—where's it taking you?	Pick a time or place.	80s Miami—neon vibes and retro jams. (15 words)
119	What's a fake app you'd create to fix boredom?	Invent something wild or useful.	VibeGenix—sparks instant story ideas with one tap. (15 words)
120	If you could talk to an animal, what would it say?	Pick an animal and give it attitude.	My dog says, "Feed me, then we conquer." (15 words)
121	What's one thing you'd change about today to spark ideas?	Remix your day for creativity.	Add a random dance break to shake off stress. (15 words)

Flowchart: Block Buster Vibes (Doodle this in your notebook!)

Imagine this as a colorful flowchart to map your block-busting strategy. Here's a text-based version to guide your sketch:

```
                          [Crush the Block]
                                 |
              ----------------------------------------
              |            |            |            |
        [What's Stuck]  [Quick Fix]  [Silly Idea]  [Next Spark]
              |            |            |            |
         Why I'm stuck   Try a fix  Write something  Idea to keep
         (e.g., stress) (e.g., music) wild or dumb    going
```

How to Use It: Start at "Crush the Block" and branch out. Write one idea for each—like why you're stuck or a silly idea to try. Add neon pens or stickers to make it pop!

Play to Spark Confidence 🎲

Now that you're busting blocks like a champ, let's make writing a game to keep your confidence soaring. This section's got Prompts #122–139: Playful Sparks to turn writing into playtime, plus Prompts #140–156: Recovery Sparks to get you back on track after a block. We'll also throw in a quiz to figure out your block-busting style. Let's make creativity fun again!

Exercise: Idea Dump & Quick Shape

Prompt: "Dump all your random thoughts, then shape one into a mini-story."
Assignment: Jot down 5 random thoughts in 2 minutes (words, images, anything). Pick one and turn it into a 50-word story snippet.
Sample Answer: Thoughts: neon lights, tacos, jetpack, rain, meme. Story: I jetpack over a rainy city, neon lights glowing below. Tacos fuel my mission to deliver the ultimate meme to a secret rebel base. (50 words)
TikTok Idea: Film with a neon filter, "Jetpack Joyride" sound, and text like "Tacos + Memes = Epic."

Prompts #122–139: Playful Sparks

These prompts are like a creative playground—fun, silly, and designed to get you writing without overthinking. Perfect for crushing blocks with a smile.

Prompt #	Prompt	Hint	Sample Answer
122	Your shoe's a spaceship—where's it going?	Turn something ordinary into sci-fi.	My sneaker rockets to a neon galaxy party. (15 words)
123	Write a one-line rap about your day.	Spit bars about your vibe.	Yo, I'm slaying school, my ideas stay cool. (15 words)
124	Your lunch is alive—what's it saying?	Give your food some attitude.	My sandwich yells, "Eat me, I'm your MVP!" (15 words)
125	If you were a cartoon, what's your goofy catchphrase?	Make it silly and iconic.	"Oops, I vibed too hard again!" (15 words)
126	Your favorite game character crashes your day—what happens?	Pick a character and go wild.	Mario joins my class, teaching jumps over homework. (15 words)
127	What's a fake holiday you'd invent?	Create a fun day to celebrate.	Meme Day—share memes, no work allowed. (15 words)
128	Your pencil's a magic wand—what's it do?	Give it a magical power.	Draws portals to a candy-filled dimension. (15 words)
129	If your life was a board game, what's one rule?	Make it fun or quirky.	Roll a six, get a snack break. (15 words)
130	You're a superhero with a silly power—what is it?	Think weird but useful.	I turn frowns into glitter explosions. (15 words)
131	Your favorite song's a story—what's the plot?	Turn lyrics into a mini-tale.	"Levitating" by Dua Lipa: I float through a neon city. (15 words)
132	What's a toy you'd bring to life?	Pick a toy and give it personality.	My plushie bear becomes a sassy adventure guide. (15 words)
133	You're a game show host—what's the prize?	Dream up a wild reward.	A lifetime supply of custom sneakers. (15 words)
134	Your homework's a monster—what's it look like?	Make it scary or funny.	Math homework's a dragon with equation scales. (15 words)
135	What's a fake ad you'd make for a random object?	Sell something boring in a fun way.	Glow-in-the-dark eraser—erase mistakes with style! (15 words)
136	You're a pirate—what's your ship's name?	Give it a bold, pirate-y vibe.	The Neon Kraken—fastest ship in the galaxy. (15 words)
137	Your favorite emoji's alive—what's it do?	Pick an emoji and make it wild.	😎 throws epic parties with glowing sunglasses. (15 words)
138	What's a dance move you'd invent?	Create a move that's all you.	The Vibe Spin—twirl with neon flair. (15 words)
139	Your room's a movie set—what's the film?	Describe the vibe of the movie.	Cyberpunk thriller with glowing lights and secrets. (15 words)

Quiz: Block Buster Type

Take this quick quiz to find your block-busting style! (Picture this with fun checkboxes and emojis!)

1. What's stopping your writing vibe?
   - A) Overthinking—my ideas feel lame. 😬
   - B) Stress—life's too chaotic. 😟
   - C) Boredom—nothing feels exciting. 😴
   - D) I'm good, just need a spark! 🚀
2. What gets you hyped to create?
   - A) Music or a dope playlist. 🎵
   - B) A funny or silly vibe. 😜
   - C) A quick, random challenge. ⚡
   - D) Daydreaming or gaming. 🎮
3. What's your go-to when you're stuck?
   - A) Doodle or scribble anything. ✏️
   - B) Talk it out with a friend. 💬
   - C) Take a break and vibe. 😎
   - D) Try a new creative outlet. 🌟

Solutions:

- Mostly A's: You're a Vibe Shifter. Use music or quick prompts (like #122–139) to spark ideas.
- Mostly B's: You're a Playful Creator. Try silly prompts (#122–139) to laugh past blocks.
- Mostly C's: You're a Quick Fixer. Use fast sparks (#105–121) for instant wins.
- Mostly D's: You're a Dream Weaver. Recovery sparks (#140–156) will get you back in the game.

Prompts #140–156: Recovery Sparks

These prompts are your comeback crew, helping you recover from a block and get back to creating with confidence. They're designed to ease you back into the flow.

Prompt	Prompt	Hint	Sample Answer
140	What's one thing you love doing that sparks ideas?	Think about a hobby or vibe.	Gaming—building Minecraft worlds inspires epic stories. (15 words)
141	If you could ditch one stress, what is it?	Pick something weighing you down.	Homework stress—more time for creative vibes. (15 words)
142	Your dream escape is a story—what's the setting?	Imagine a place to chill.	Floating island with glowing trees and music. (15 words)
143	What's a compliment you'd give your creativity?	Hype up your brain!	"You turn random thoughts into pure fire!" (15 words)
144	If your block was a villain, who is it?	Give it a name and vibe.	The Overthinker—steals ideas with doubt clouds. (15 words)
145	What's a song that gets you unstuck?	Pick a track that lifts you.	"Good 4 U" by Olivia Rodrigo—pure energy boost. (15 words)
146	You're a wizard—what spell breaks your block?	Create a magical fix.	IdeaStorm—summons a shower of random thoughts. (15 words)
147	What's a memory that makes you smile?	Pick a happy moment for inspo.	Laughing with friends at a summer bonfire. (15 words)
148	Your favorite character cheers you up—what do they	Pick a character from a show or game.	Spider-Man: "Swing through the block, you got this!" (15 words)
149	What's a place you'd write in to feel free?	Imagine your ideal writing spot.	Rooftop with city lights and a chill breeze. (15 words)
150	If your ideas were a drink, what are they?	Create a drink that's your vibe.	Neon energy drink—sparkly, bold, and unstoppable. (15 words)
151	What's a quick win you can celebrate today?	Find a small victory to hype.	Wrote one sentence—boom, I'm back! (15 words)
152	Your block's a monster—what defeats it?	Imagine a way to slay it.	Laughter—a goofy idea crushes it instantly. (15 words)
153	What's a random word that sparks a story?	Pick a word and run with it.	"Glow"—a city powered by neon dreams. (15 words)
154	If you could borrow a friend's vibe, whose is it?	Pick a friend's energy to steal.	Jaden's chill confidence—makes writing feel easy. (15 words)
155	What's a fake headline about your comeback?	Write a bold, fun headline.	"Teen Crushes Block with Epic Idea Storm!" (15 words)
156	What's one thing you're excited to write next?	Look forward to your next spark.	A sci-fi TikTok script about time travel. (15 words)

Monthly Check-In #3: Quick Reflection Grid

Take 2 minutes at the end of the month to vibe-check your progress. Fill out this grid in your journal! (Picture a colorful table with emoji headers!)

Question	Your Answer	Emoji Vibe
What's one prompt that crushed your block?		😍
What's a win you're proud of this month?		💪
What was the toughest block to beat?		😬
What's your next creative spark?		🚀

Example:

Loved: Prompt #105—describing my sneakers sparked a story! 😍
Proud: Wrote through a stress block—huge win! 💪
Tough: Overthinking my ideas was rough. 😬
Next: Try a playful prompt for a TikTok! 🚀

Keep Crushing It! 🚀

You're a block-busting legend with these 52 prompts, turning stuck moments into creative wins. Whether it's a quick spark or a playful vibe, you've got the tools to keep your ideas flowing. Ready for more? Flip to Chapter 4 to level up your storytelling skills and make your creativity shine brighter than ever. Your brain's unstoppable—let's keep it lit!

ACTIVITY ZONE

ACTIVITY 1 – BLOCK-BUSTING BRAINSTORM

Prompt: "Dump every random idea in your head to spark something new."

Assignment: Write down 5 random words or thoughts in 2 minutes (anything goes—colors, objects, vibes). Pick one and write a 25-word story snippet based on it.

Questions:
1. What's the first random word or thought that pops into your head?
2. What's a second word or thought—go wild!
3. What's a third word or thought, no matter how weird?
4. Pick one of your words/thoughts—what's a quick story vibe it sparks?
5. Write a 10-word caption to share your story snippet on TikTok.

ACTIVITY 2 – BLOCK-BUSTING BRAINSTORM

Prompt: "Take a boring or stressful moment and flip it into something fun."

Questions:
1. What's a boring or stressful moment from today (e.g., homework, waiting)?
2. If it was a movie scene, what genre would you make it?
3. What's one detail you'd add to make it epic (e.g., music, setting)?
4. Who's the hero of this flipped moment—you or someone else?
5. Pitch it as a 10-word Instagram caption.

🎯 ACTIVITY ZONE

ACTIVITY 3 – SILLY SPARK GENERATOR

Prompt: "Turn something totally random into a goofy story starter."
Questions:
1. Pick a random object nearby—what is it?
2. Give it a silly superpower—what can it do?
3. Where's this object's adventure happening (e.g., school, space)?
4. What's one line this object says in your story?
5. Describe it in a 10-word group chat message to hype your friends.

ACTIVITY 4 – CONFIDENCE COMEBACK

Prompt: "Hype yourself up to crush a creative block."
Questions:
1. What's one thing you're awesome at creatively (e.g., humor, imagination)?
2. How did you use that strength recently, even in a small way?
3. What's a block you've beaten before (e.g., a tough day)?
4. What's a pep-talk phrase you'd tell yourself to keep going?
5. How would you flex this on TikTok (sound, vibe, text)?

ANSWERS
🎯 ACTIVITY ZONE

(Use these to spark ideas, but make your answers 100% you!)

Exercise 1: Block-Busting Brainstorm
1. Cloud.
2. Skateboard.
3. Glitter.
4. Glitter sparks a story about a sparkling alien invasion. Story: Glitter rains from the sky, turning my town into a glowing alien disco. I skate through, dodging sparkly invaders with my crew. (25 words)
5. "Glitter aliens invade—skate or sparkle! # Blockbuster"

Exercise 2: Vibe Flip
1. Waiting for the bus was boring.
2. Action—think Mission: Impossible.
3. Neon rain and a "Savage" by Megan Thee Stallion soundtrack.
4. Me, the rogue agent.
5. "Bus stop turned epic mission—neon vibes only!"

Exercise 3: Silly Spark Generator
1. My water bottle.
2. It can sing pop songs to inspire courage.
3. In a futuristic school cafeteria.
4. "Yo, drink me and sing to win!"
5. "My water bottle sings bangers—cafeteria chaos!"

Exercise 4: Confidence Comeback
1. I'm awesome at creating funny TikTok scripts.
2. Made my friends laugh with a meme-inspired skit.
3. Beat a block when I was stressed about finals.
4. "You're a creative beast—keep slaying those ideas!"
5. Use "Industry Baby" by Lil Nas X, neon filter, text: "Crushing blocks with fire ideas!"

Chapter 4. Idea Playground – Fun Genre Sparks for Every Mood ✍

CHAPTER 4 – Idea Playground – Fun Genre Sparks for Every Mood ✍️

Yo, what's good? You've been killing it through Chapters 1–3, owning your ideas, building daily habits, and smashing writer's block like a pro. Now, welcome to Chapter 4 of 365 Writing Prompts for Teens, where we're diving into the Idea Playground! This chapter's packed with 53 prompts to spark your creativity across genres like fantasy, sci-fi, and everyday vibes, no matter what mood you're in. Whether you're dreaming of epic quests or vibing with real-life feels, these prompts, tables, and exercises will keep your ideas flowing like a viral TikTok. Ready to play? Let's jump in! 🚀

Fantasy & Sci-Fi Quick Adventures 🎲

Ready to escape into worlds of dragons, spaceships, or neon-lit futures? This section's all about sparking epic adventures with Prompts #157–173: Fantasy & Sci-Fi Sparks. These are perfect for when you're craving something bold, wild, and out-of-this-world. Let's get your imagination soaring!

Table: Genre Spark Guide

This table breaks down fantasy and sci-fi vibes to match your mood, with quick tips to get you writing.

Mood	Genre Vibe	Quick Tip
Feeling epic?	High Fantasy	Imagine a quest with dragons or magic—add one bold hero!
Want something futuristic?	Sci-Fi Adventure	Picture neon cities or AI battles—throw in a tech twist.
Craving mystery?	Dark Fantasy	Add a creepy forest or cursed artifact for suspense.
Need a quick escape?	Space Opera	Write about a starship crew facing a galactic crisis.

Mindmap: Epic Adventure Vibe (Doodle this in your notebook!)

Imagine this as a colorful flowchart to map your fantasy/sci-fi ideas. Here's a text-based version to guide your sketch:

```
                          [Epic Adventure]
                                 |
        -----------------------------------------
        |              |              |              |
[Hero's Quest]  [World Vibe]  [Big Twist]  [Cool Gadget/Magic]
        |              |              |              |
Main character's  Setting      Plot surprise   A tool or spell
   mission      (e.g., neon city) (e.g., betrayal) (e.g., laser sword)
```

How to Use It: Start at "Epic Adventure" and branch out. Write one idea for each—like a hero's mission or a magical gadget. Add stickers or neon pens to make it pop!

Prompts #157–173: Fantasy & Sci-Fi Sparks

These prompts are your ticket to wild, imaginative worlds. They're quick, fun, and designed to spark epic stories in minutes. Here's the full list with hints and sample answers.

Prompt #	Prompt	Hint	Sample Answer
157	You're a dragon rider—what's your dragon's name and power?	Name your dragon and give it a cool ability.	Blaze, breathes neon flames that light up the sky. (15 words)
158	Your spaceship crashes on a strange planet—what's it like?	Describe a wild, alien world.	Glowing purple jungles with floating islands and singing vines. (15 words)
159	You find a magic amulet—what does it do?	Give it a unique power.	Grants invisibility but only when you're super confident. (15 words)
160	You're a time-traveling knight—where do you go?	Pick a time or place for your quest.	Future Tokyo, battling robots with a glowing sword. (15 words)
161	Your phone's an AI with attitude—what's it say?	Give your phone a sassy sci-fi vibe.	"Upgrade your ideas, human—I'm bored of TikTok." (15 words)
162	You're a wizard's apprentice—what's your first spell?	Create a spell that's all you.	VibeBolt—shoots sparks that inspire epic ideas. (15 words)
163	Your pet's a sci-fi sidekick—what's their role?	Turn your pet into a techy helper.	My cat hacks enemy drones with laser eyes. (15 words)
164	You're in a fantasy tavern—who do you meet?	Describe a mysterious character.	A cloaked elf with secrets about a cursed crown. (15 words)

Prompt #	Prompt	Hint	Sample Answer
165	Your backpack's a portal—where does it lead?	Pick a magical or futuristic destination.	A neon-lit city with floating skateparks. (15 words)
166	You're a rebel in a dystopian city—what's your mission?	Create a bold, sci-fi goal.	Hack the city's AI to free trapped dreamers. (15 words)
167	Your shoes are enchanted—what do they do?	Give them a magical power.	Run at lightspeed, leaving glowing trails behind. (15 words)
168	You're a space pirate—what's your ship's name?	Name your ship with swagger.	StarVibe—fastest ship stealing galactic treasures. (15 words)
169	You find a cursed book—what's its secret?	Describe a dark fantasy twist.	It traps readers in a shadowy dream realm. (15 words)
170	Your bestie's a robot—what's their quirk?	Give them a fun or weird trait.	JadenBot glitches into dance mode randomly. (15 words)
171	You're a mage—what's your signature magic?	Create a spell that's your vibe.	GlowWave—lights up allies with confidence boosts. (15 words)
172	Your skateboard's a sci-fi gadget—what does it do?	Turn it into a futuristic tool.	Hovers through wormholes for instant travel. (15 words)
173	You're a hero in a fantasy world—what's your weapon?	Pick a weapon that screams you.	A neon whip that sparks with energy. (15 words)

Everyday Sparks & Emotions 🌈

Not every story needs dragons or spaceships—sometimes the realest vibes come from everyday life and big feels. This section's got Prompts #174–191: Emotional Sparks to tap into your emotions and Prompts #192–209: Poetry & Social Sparks to share your vibe with the world. Plus, a quiz to match your mood to the perfect genre. Let's get personal and playful!

Exercise: Routine-to-Magic

Prompt: "Turn a daily routine into a magical or epic moment."

Assignment: Pick a boring routine (like brushing your teeth) and write a 50-word story snippet that makes it fantastical or emotional.

Sample Answer: Brushing my teeth, I'm a sorcerer cleansing a cursed mirror. Each stroke banishes shadows, revealing a glowing portal to a neon realm of dreams. (50 words)

TikTok Idea: Film brushing with a sparkly filter, "Magic" by B.o.B as the sound, and text like "Brushing away curses!"

Mindmap: Emotional Vibe (Sketch this in your notebook!)

Imagine this as a vibrant flowchart to map your everyday emotions. Here's a text-based version to guide your doodle:

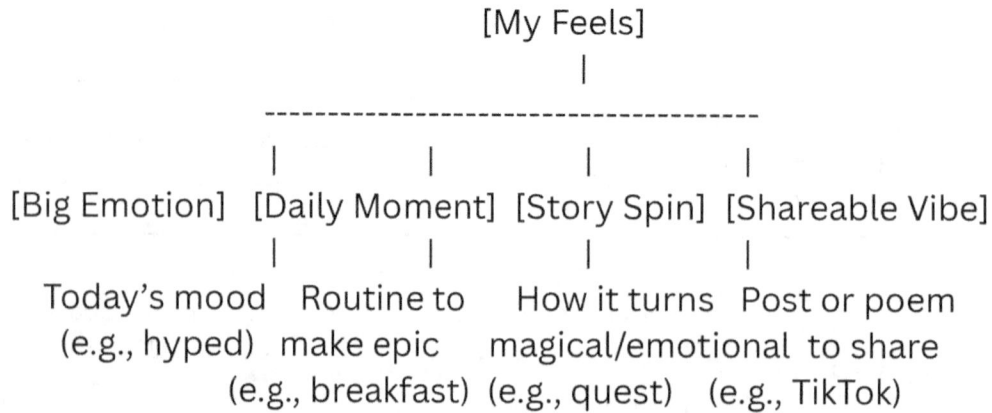

How to Use It: Start at "My Feels" and branch out. Write one idea for each—like a mood or a routine turned epic. Add colors or stickers to make it fire!

Prompts #174–191: Emotional Sparks

These prompts dig into your feelings—happy, stressed, hyped, or chill—to spark stories that feel real. They're perfect for turning everyday moments into something deep.

Prompt #	Prompt	Hint	Sample Answer
174	What's a moment today that made you smile?	Pick a happy memory and describe it.	My friend's dumb joke at lunch had me crying laughing. (15 words)
175	You're stressed—what's a story to escape it?	Imagine a calming tale.	I hide in a forest where trees sing lullabies. (15 words)
176	What's a memory that feels like a warm hug?	Think of a cozy moment.	Chilling with my dog, watching the sunset glow. (15 words)
177	You're hyped—what's sparking your energy?	Capture that high vibe.	Crushed a test—feeling like I'm unstoppable today! (15 words)
178	What's a moment you felt super proud?	Celebrate a win, big or small.	Got my TikTok to 100 likes—pure flex! (15 words)
179	You're sad—what's a story to lift you up?	Create a hopeful tale.	A rainbow bird leads me to a glowing city. (15 words)
180	What's a time you felt unstoppable?	Relive a boss moment.	Skated a new trick perfectly—crowd cheered! (15 words)
181	Your anger's a character—what do they do?	Turn anger into a story figure.	RedFlare, smashing obstacles with fiery punches. (15 words)
182	What's a chill moment you want to relive?	Pick a relaxed vibe.	Vibing to music, sprawled on my bed. (15 words)

Prompt #	Prompt	Hint	Sample Answer
183	You're nervous—what's a story to calm you?	Imagine a soothing scene.	Floating on a cloud with soft starlight. (15 words)
184	What's a time you helped a friend?	Share a kind moment.	Helped Mia study—her smile was worth it. (15 words)
185	Your happiness is a place—where is it?	Describe a joyful setting.	Neon beach with waves dancing to my playlist. (15 words)
186	What's a moment you felt misunderstood?	Dig into that feeling.	Nobody got my art project—it's my vibe, though! (15 words)
187	You're excited—what's the big thing?	Capture your hype.	Got tickets to a concert—gonna lose it! (15 words)
188	Your boredom's a story—what happens?	Turn boredom into adventure.	Boredom monster traps me; I escape via jetpack. (15 words)
189	What's a time you felt super connected?	Think of a bond moment.	Group chat blowing up with meme wars—epic. (15 words)
190	Your fear's a creature—what is it?	Give fear a wild form.	ShadowWolf—chases me but I outrun it. (15 words)
191	What's a dream you want to chase?	Share a big goal.	Make a viral TikTok series about my life. (15 words)

Quiz: Genre Spark Match

Take this quick quiz to find the genre that matches your vibe! (Picture this with fun checkboxes and emojis!)

(1) What's your mood right now?
A) Hyped and ready to slay! 🚀
B) Chill, just vibing. 😎
C) Deep in my feels. 😢
D) Want something wild and weird. 🤪

(2) What's your go-to creative vibe?
A) Epic battles or quests. ⚔️
B) Real-life moments with a twist. ⭐
C) Emotional stories or poems. ✒️
D) Funny or random ideas. 😂

(3) What sparks your ideas best?
A) Movies or games like Star Wars. 🎮
B) Everyday life or TikTok trends. 📱
C) Your feelings or memories. 💭
D) Random, silly thoughts. 🤪

Solutions:
Mostly A's: You're a Fantasy/Sci-Fi Star. Dive into Prompts #157–173 for epic vibes.
Mostly B's: You're an Everyday Alchemist. Try Prompts #174–191 for real-life sparks.
Mostly C's: You're a Heartfelt Poet. Use Prompts #192–209 for emotional depth.
Mostly D's: You're a Playful Maverick. Mix and match any prompt for fun!

Prompts #192–209: Poetry & Social Sparks

These prompts are designed to help you turn your vibes into poetry or shareable social media moments. They're perfect for quick, creative bursts that connect with your crew or followers.

Prompt #	Prompt	Hint	Sample Answer
192	Write a 5-word poem about your day.	Sum up your vibe poetically.	Neon dreams, chaos, still slaying. (5 words)
193	Your mood's a TikTok—what's the sound?	Pick a trending sound for your vibe.	"Savage" by Megan Thee Stallion—bold. (15 words)
194	Write a one-line poem about a friend.	Capture their vibe poetically.	Jaden's laugh lights up stars. (15 words)
195	Your life's a hashtag—what is it?	Create a shareable tag.	#GlowChaser—living for epic moments. (15 words)
196	Write a 5-word poem about a dream.	Dream big in few words.	Flying high, chasing neon skies. (5 words)

Prompt #	Prompt	Hint	Sample Answer
197	Your favorite place is a poem—what's it like?	Turn a place into poetry.	City pulses, lights sing freedom. (15 words)
198	What's a TikTok caption for your mood?	Make it short and viral.	"Vibing hard, no stress allowed." (15 words)
199	Write a one-line poem about hope.	Keep it simple and uplifting.	Stars whisper, tomorrow's gonna shine. (15 words)
200	Your squad's a poem—what's the vibe?	Capture your crew's energy.	We're sparks, igniting wild dreams. (15 words)
201	What's a tweet about your day?	Sum it up in 280 characters.	"Crushed school, vibed to Drake. #Mood" (15 words)
202	Write a 5-word poem about a memory.	Pick a moment that sticks.	Summer nights, laughter, endless stars. (5 words)
203	Your stress is a poem—what's it say?	Turn stress into art.	Heavy clouds, but I'll break through. (15 words)
204	What's a caption for a vibe selfie?	Make it bold or chill.	"Slaying today, glowing always." (15 words)
205	Write a one-line poem about joy.	Capture pure happiness.	Sunlight dances, my heart soars. (15 words)
206	Your phone's a poem—what's its voice?	Give it poetic swagger.	I buzz, connecting dreams to stars. (15 words)
207	What's a TikTok trend you'd start?	Create a viral-worthy idea.	Neon poetry slams with glow sticks. (15 words)
208	Write a 5-word poem about your future.	Dream big for tomorrow.	Bold moves, bright lights, unstoppable. (5 words)
209	Your vibe's a social post—what's it say?	Make it shareable and you.	"Chasing dreams, sparking vibes. #LiveLoud" (15 words)

Monthly Check-In #4: Quick Reflection Grid

Take 2 minutes at the end of the month to vibe-check your progress. Fill out this grid in your journal! (Picture a colorful table with emoji headers!)

Question	Your Answer	Emoji Vibe
What's one prompt you loved?		😍
What's a genre you vibed with?		🌀
What was tough to write?		😬
What's your next creative goal?		🚀

Keep the Playground Vibes Going! 🚀

You're a genre-sparking legend with these 53 prompts, turning every mood into a creative win. From fantasy quests to emotional poems, you've got the tools to make your ideas pop off. Ready for more? Flip to Chapter 5 to remix your stories and take your creativity to the next level. Your playground's open—keep it lit!

🎯 ACTIVITY ZONE

ACTIVITY 1: FANTASY FLASH

Prompt: Create a mini-fantasy story from a random spark.

Questions:
1. Pick a random object nearby—what is it?
2. Give it a magical power—what does it do?
3. Where's this story happening (e.g., forest, castle)?
4. Who's the hero—you or someone else?
5. Pitch it as a 10-word TikTok caption.

ACTIVITY 2: SCI-FI SNAP

Prompt: Turn a daily moment into a sci-fi adventure.

Questions:

1. What's a daily moment from today (e.g., eating breakfast)?
2. What's a futuristic twist you'd add?
3. What's one detail that makes it epic (e.g., tech, setting)?
4. What's one line your character says?
5. Describe it in a 10-word Instagram caption.

🎯 ACTIVITY ZONE

ACTIVITY 3: EMOTIONAL BURST

Prompt: Write a short story or poem based on a feeling.

Questions:
1. What's a strong emotion you felt today?
2. What's a setting that matches that emotion?
3. What's one image or detail that captures it?
4. What's a line that sums up the vibe?
5. Pitch it as a 10-word social media post.

ACTIVITY 4: SOCIAL VIBE SHARE

Prompt: Turn a prompt into a shareable social media moment.

Questions:
1. Which prompt from this chapter sparked you?
2. What's the vibe of your post (epic, emotional, funny)?
3. What platform would you share it on (e.g., TikTok, Insta)?
4. What's one visual element (filter, sound, etc.)?
5. Write a 10-word caption for the post.

ANSWERS
🎯 ACTIVITY ZONE

(Use these to spark ideas, but make your answers 100% you!)

ACTIVITY 1 – FANTASY FLASH

1. My water bottle.
2. It summons glowing water spirits.
3. Enchanted forest with misty rivers.
4. Me, the spirit tamer.
5. "Water bottle summons epic spirits! #FantasyVibes"

ACTIVITY 2 – SCI-FI SNAP

1. Eating breakfast.
2. My cereal's an AI energy source.
3. Holographic kitchen with floating spoons.
4. "This cereal powers my starship!"
5. "Breakfast fuels my galactic mission!"

ACTIVITY 3 – EMOTIONAL BURST

1. Happiness.
2. Sunny beach with glowing waves.
3. Sparkling sand under my feet.
4. "Joy flows like waves tonight."
5. "Happiness shines on glowing shores."

ACTIVITY 4 – SOCIAL VIBE SHARE

1. Prompt #192—5-word poem about my day.
2. Chill and poetic vibe.
3. TikTok.
4. Starry filter with "Dreams" by Fleetwood Mac.
5. "Neon dreams, chaos, still slaying."

Chapter 5. Spark Your Voice – Easy Ways to Sound Like You

CHAPTER 5 – Spark Your Voice – Easy Ways to Sound Like You

Yo, what's good? You've been owning your ideas, building habits, crushing writer's block, and playing with genres like a creative legend in Chapters 1-4. Now, welcome to Chapter 5 of 365 Writing Prompts for Teens, where it's all about finding your voice—the unique vibe that makes your writing scream you. With 52 prompts, this chapter's got quick, fun ways to make your words pop like a viral TikTok and build confidence in your style. Whether you're hyping your squad or sharing your truth, these prompts will help you sound 100% authentic. Ready to let your voice shine? Let's dive in! 🚀

Why Your Voice Builds Confidence 🎤

Your voice is your superpower—it's how you tell the world who you are. This section's all about sparking that voice with Prompts #210-226: Voice Sparks, designed to help you write like you talk, vibe, and dream. No fake stuff here—just your raw, real energy turned into words.

Table: Voice Spark Builder

This table breaks down ways to find your voice and make it shine, no matter your mood or style.

Vibe	Voice Trick	Why It Works
Chill & Real	Write like you're texting your bestie.	Keeps it natural, like a group chat vibe.
Bold & Hype	Use big, loud words or slang you love.	Makes your writing feel like a flex.
Deep & Feels	Dig into emotions—happy, sad, or chaotic.	Connects your heart to your words.
Funny & Quirky	Add memes, jokes, or random humor.	Shows off your unique personality.

Quick Tip: Not sure where to start? Say, "My voice is fire because it's mine." Stick it on a note by your desk to remind you to stay grounded.

Workflow: Voice Quick Lab ⚡

Here's a 5-minute plan to spark your voice and make your writing sound like you. (Picture this as a dope flowchart in your journal!)

Start → [Pick a Vibe] → [Choose Prompt] → [Write 3 mins] → [Read Aloud] → [Tweak or Share]

1. Pick a Vibe: Choose a vibe from the table above (e.g., chill, bold).
2. Choose a prompt from the table below or flip to a random page.
3. Write (3 mins): Jot down whatever flows, like you're talking to your crew.
4. Read Aloud: Say it out loud—does it sound like you?
5. Tweak or Share: Polish it or drop it in a TikTok or group chat.

Pro Tip: Blast a song that matches your vibe (like "Montero" by Lil Nas X for bold) to get in the zone while you write.

Mindmap: Your Voice Vibe (Doodle this in your notebook!)

Imagine this as a colorful flowchart to map your unique voice. Here's a text-based version to guide your sketch:

```
                        [My Voice]
                            |
         ---------------------------------------
         |           |           |           |
    [My Slang]  [My Feels]  [My Humor]  [My Story]
         |           |           |           |
    Words I use  Emotions I   Jokes or    What I want
    (e.g., "lit") vibe with   memes I love  to share
                 (e.g., hyped) (e.g., goofy) (e.g., truth)
```

How to Use It: Start at "My Voice" and branch out. Write one idea for each—like a slang word you love or a story you want to tell. Add neon pens or stickers to make it pop!

Prompts #210–226: Voice Sparks

These prompts are all about finding your unique style—your slang, your feels, your vibe. They're quick, fun, and designed to make your words sound like you. Here's the full list with hints and sample answers.

Prompt #	Prompt	Hint	Sample Answer
210	Write a sentence using your favorite slang word.	Pick a word you say all the time.	Yo, this vibe's straight-up lit! (15 words)
211	Describe your day like you're texting your bestie.	Keep it chill and real.	Dude, school was chaos, but I'm vibing now. (15 words)
212	What's a catchphrase that's so you?	Make it bold or funny.	"Slay now, stress later!" (15 words)
213	Your mood's a story—what's the opening line?	Capture your vibe today.	I'm hyped, ready to conquer galaxies! (15 words)
214	Write a one-line rant about something annoying.	Let it out, keep it you.	Homework's stealing my vibe—ugh, why?! (15 words)
215	What's a truth you'd shout to the world?	Be real and bold.	I'm me, and that's enough! (15 words)
216	Describe your dream hangout spot in your voice.	Use your style to paint it.	Neon arcade, loud music, pure chaos—my spot! (15 words)
217	Your life's a meme—what's the caption?	Make it funny or relatable.	"When life hits, I vibe harder." (15 words)
218	Write a line as if you're a movie narrator.	Use your dramatic or chill voice.	In a world where I slay… (15 words)

Prompt #	Prompt	Hint	Sample Answer
219	What's a compliment you'd give yourself?	Hype your unique vibe.	Yo, my ideas are straight fire! (15 words)
220	Your favorite song's a story—what's your line?	Use your voice to add to it.	I'm dancing through neon dreams tonight. (15 words)
221	What's a word that feels like you?	Pick one that's your vibe.	"Spark"—I'm all about igniting ideas. (15 words)
222	Write a one-line hype speech for your crew.	Motivate them in your style.	Yo, squad, let's own this vibe! (15 words)
223	Your room's a character—what's its voice?	Give it your personality.	Yo, I'm chill but full of secrets. (15 words)
224	What's a fake ad for your personality?	Sell yourself in your voice.	GlowVibe: Unleash your inner spark daily! (15 words)
225	Your life's a TikTok—what's the vibe?	Describe your viral moment.	Dancing through chaos with neon energy. (15 words)
226	Write a one-line poem in your voice.	Keep it short and you.	I'm a spark, lighting up dreams. (15 words)

Risk Sparks & Bold Ideas 🔥

Now that you're finding your voice, let's get bold! This section's about taking risks with your writing, mixing styles, and sharing your vibe with the world. With Prompts #227–244: Style Mixes and Prompts #245–261: Share-Ready Sparks, plus a quiz to boost your confidence, you'll be ready to let your voice shine loud and proud.

Exercise: Bold Idea Try

Prompt: "Take a risk with a bold, unique story idea in your voice."

Assignment: Write a 50-word story snippet that feels daring—mix genres, use your slang, or go wild.

Sample Answer: Yo, I'm a neon ninja in a cyber-fantasy city, slicing through digital dragons with my glow-stick katana. My squad's hyped, dropping "lit" in the chat. (50 words)

TikTok Idea: Film with a cyberpunk filter, "Industry Baby" by Lil Nas X, and text like "Ninja vibes only!"

Mindmap: Bold Voice Vibe (Sketch this in your notebook!)

Imagine this as a vibrant flowchart to map your bold ideas. Here's a text-based version to guide your doodle:

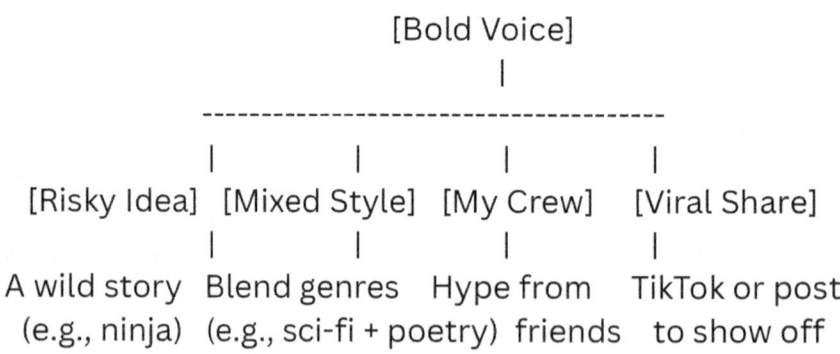

How to Use It: Start at "Bold Voice" and branch out. Write one idea for each—like a risky story or a mixed-genre vibe. Add stickers or neon colors to make it fire!

Prompts #227–244: Style Mixes

These prompts push you to mix genres, vibes, or styles to create something totally you. They're perfect for taking risks and finding new ways to express your voice.

66

Prompt #	Prompt	Hint	Sample Answer
227	Mix sci-fi and poetry—what's your line?	Blend futuristic vibes with feels.	Stars hum my name in code. (15 words)
228	Write a fantasy story as a text convo.	Use your texting style.	Yo, dragon's attacking—grab the sword! 🗡 (15 words)
229	Your life's a comedy skit—what's the punchline?	Make it funny in your voice.	"Oops, I vibed too hard!" (15 words)
230	Mix a meme with a sci-fi vibe.	Combine internet humor with futurism.	Distracted Boyfriend meme, but with spaceships. (15 words)
231	Write a horror story in your chill voice.	Keep it spooky but you.	Yo, that ghost's just vibing wrong. (15 words)
232	Your day's a rap—what's the first line?	Spit bars in your style.	Yo, I'm slaying school, no stress. (15 words)
233	Mix romance and adventure—what's the vibe?	Blend love with epic action.	Kissing under stars, dodging lasers. (15 words)
234	Write a mystery in your bold voice.	Solve a case with swagger.	Yo, who stole my neon vibes? (15 words)
235	Your pet's a fantasy character—what's their line?	Give them a magical voice.	My cat says, "Bow to meow!" (15 words)
236	Mix comedy and sci-fi—what's the scene?	Make it funny and futuristic.	My robot therapist keeps glitching mid-joke. (15 words)
237	Write a poem as a group chat.	Use your texting vibe.	Yo, stars shine, we vibe—bet! (15 words)
238	Your life's a game show—what's the name?	Create a bold, you-inspired show.	Vibe Clash: Win with Swagger. (15 words)
239	Mix fantasy and your favorite slang.	Use your words in a magical world.	This dragon's straight-up yeeted! (15 words)
240	Write a sci-fi story as a meme caption.	Keep it short and viral.	"When your spaceship's lowkey sus." (15 words)
241	Your mood's a thriller—what's the twist?	Add suspense in your voice.	Yo, my shadow's plotting against me! (15 words)
242	Mix poetry and adventure—what's the line?	Blend epic quests with feels.	Sword in hand, heart beats loud. (15 words)
243	Your friend's a comic villain—what's their plan?	Make it bold and funny.	Mia steals vibes with glitter bombs. (15 words)
244	Write a fantasy tale as a TikTok script.	Use your voice for viral vibes.	Yo, I slay dragons—follow me! (15 words)

Quiz: Voice Confidence Boost

Take this quick quiz to level up your voice confidence! (Picture this with fun checkboxes and emojis!)

1. What's your writing vibe right now?
   - A) Bold and loud, let's go! 🚀
   - B) Chill, just keeping it real. 😎
   - C) Deep and emotional. 🥺
   - D) Funny and a little chaotic. 😂
2. What makes your voice pop?
   - A) Slang or hype phrases. 💨
   - B) Real talk, like texting. 💬
   - C) Feels or poetic vibes. ✍️
   - D) Jokes or random humor. 😜
3. What's holding your voice back?
   - A) Worried it's not "cool" enough. 😬
   - B) Hard to sound like me. 🤔
   - C) Scared to share my feels. 😟
   - D) I'm good, just want bolder vibes! ⭐

Solutions:

- Mostly A's: You're a Hype Master. Use Prompts #227–244 for bold style mixes.
- Mostly B's: You're a Real Talker. Try Prompts #210–226 for chill voice vibes.
- Mostly C's: You're a Heartfelt Viber. Dive into Prompts #245–261 for share-ready feels.
- Mostly D's: You're a Chaos Creator. Mix and match any prompt for fun!

Prompts #245–261: Share-Ready Sparks

These prompts are designed to make your voice shine in shareable ways—think TikToks, posts, or group chat flexes. They're bold, fun, and ready for the world to see.

Prompt #	Prompt	Hint	Sample Answer
245	Write a TikTok caption in your voice.	Make it viral and you.	"Vibing hard, chasing neon dreams!" (15 words)
246	Your life's a tweet—what's it say?	Sum it up in your style.	"Slaying school, sparking vibes. #GlowUp" (15 words)
247	Write a one-line poem for your bestie.	Use your voice to hype them.	Yo, you shine like neon stars. (15 words)
248	Your vibe's a group chat message—what is it?	Keep it real and fun.	Yo, squad, let's make chaos tonight! (15 words)
249	What's a hashtag for your voice?	Create a tag that's you.	#SparkVibe—bold, real, unstoppable. (15 words)
250	Write a one-line story for Insta.	Make it short and epic.	I'm a ninja, slaying doubts daily. (15 words)
251	Your mood's a meme—what's the caption?	Keep it funny and you.	"When life's tough, I vibe." (15 words)
252	Write a hype speech for your followers.	Motivate them in your voice.	Yo, chase dreams, you're unstoppable! (15 words)
253	Your day's a TikTok sound—what is it?	Pick a sound that's your vibe.	"Savage" by Megan Thee Stallion—fierce! (15 words)
254	Write a one-line poem about your dream.	Keep it poetic and you.	I'll soar through neon skies, free. (15 words)
255	Your voice's a movie—what's the title?	Name it in your style.	VibeStorm: The Rise of Me. (15 words)
256	Write a group chat roast of yourself.	Keep it light and funny.	Yo, I'm late but still lit! (15 words)
257	Your life's a post—what's the vibe?	Describe a shareable moment.	Neon nights, chasing big dreams. (15 words)
258	Write a one-line hype for your squad.	Hype them in your voice.	Squad's fire, we own the vibe! (15 words)
259	Your voice's a song—what's the chorus?	Create a lyric in your style.	Yo, I'm sparking, never stopping! (15 words)
260	Write a TikTok script in your voice.	Make it short and viral.	Yo, I'm slaying—join the vibe! (15 words)
261	Your future's a post—what's it say?	Dream big in your voice.	"Conquered dreams, living my vibe!" (15 words)

Monthly Check-In #5: Quick Reflection Grid

Take 2 minutes at the end of the month to vibe-check your progress. Fill out this grid in your journal! (Picture a colorful table with emoji headers!)

Question	Your Answer	Emoji Vibe
What's one prompt that sounded like you?		😍
What's a bold idea you tried?		💪
What was tough about finding your voice?		😬
What's your next voice goal?		🚀

Example:

- Loved: Prompt #210—my slang was fire! 😍
- Bold: Mixed sci-fi and poetry—wild! 💪
- Tough: Sounding real without overthinking. 😬
- Next: Drop a TikTok in my voice! 🚀

Keep Your Voice Lit! 🚀

You're a voice-sparking superstar with these 52 prompts, turning your slang, feels, and vibes into words that scream you. From bold style mixes to shareable posts, you've got the tools to make your voice unstoppable. Ready for more? Flip to Chapter 6 to weave your ideas into epic stories that'll blow minds. Your voice is fire—keep it blazing!

🎯 ACTIVITY ZONE

ACTIVITY 1 – SLANG SNAP

Prompt: Write a mini-story using your favorite slang.

Questions:

1. What's your go-to slang word or phrase?
2. What's the setting for your story (e.g., school, future)?
3. What's one thing that happens in your story?
4. What's a line your character says with your slang?
5. Pitch it as a 10-word TikTok caption.

ACTIVITY 2 – FEELS FLASH

Prompt: Turn a strong emotion into a story in your voice.

Questions:

1. What's a big emotion you felt today?
2. What's a setting that matches that vibe?
3. What's one detail that makes it feel real?
4. What's a line your character says in your voice?
5. Describe it in a 10-word Instagram caption.

ACTIVITY 3 – HYPE HUSTLE

Prompt: Write a bold, hype moment in your unique style.

Questions:
1. What's a moment you felt unstoppable recently?
2. What's a bold vibe for this moment (e.g., superhero, rapper)?
3. What's one detail that makes it epic?
4. What's a hype line you'd say?
5. Pitch it as a 10-word group chat message.

ACTIVITY 4 – SHAREABLE SPARK

Prompt: Create a social media post in your voice.

Questions:
1. Which prompt from this chapter inspired you?
2. What's the vibe of your post (bold, chill, funny)?
3. What platform would you share it on?
4. What's one visual element (filter, sound, etc.)?
5. Write a 10-word caption in your voice.

ANSWERS
ACTIVITY ZONE

(Use these to spark ideas, but make your answers 100% you!)

ACTIVITY 1 – SLANG SNAP

1. "Lit."
2. Neon-lit skatepark.
3. I land a trick, crowd cheers.
4. "Yo, this move's straight-up lit!"
5. "Skatepark vibes, landing lit tricks!"

ACTIVITY 2 – FEELS FLASH

1. Happiness.
2. Glowing beach at sunset.
3. Waves sparkling like my smile.
4. "Yo, I'm vibing with the sun!"
5. "Sunset glow, my heart's on fire."

ACTIVITY 3 – HYPE HUSTLE

1. Nailed a presentation in class.
2. Rapper dropping bars.
3. Spotlight hits me, crowd's hyped.
4. "Yo, I'm spitting fire today!"
5. "Crushed it, spitting bars in class!"

ACTIVITY 4 SHAREABLE SPARK

1. Prompt #245—writing a TikTok caption in my voice.
2. Bold and hype vibe.
3. TikTok.
4. Neon glow filter with "Montero" by Lil Nas X as the sound.
5. "Yo, vibing hard, sparking neon dreams daily!"

Chapter 6. : Make Ideas Pop – Fun Story Sparks in Minutes

CHAPTER 6 – : Make Ideas Pop – Fun Story Sparks in Minutes

Yo, what's up? You've been crushing it through Chapters 1–5, owning your voice, smashing blocks, and sparking ideas like a TikTok star. Now, welcome to Chapter 6 of 365 Writing Prompts for Teens, where we're turning those ideas into stories that shine! With 52 prompts, this chapter's packed with quick, fun ways to craft narratives that feel like you—from epic adventures to chill slice-of-life moments. Think characters, plots, and dialogues that pop off the page, with tables, flowcharts, and exercises to keep it fresh. Ready to make your stories unforgettable? Let's dive in! 🚀

Ideas to Quick Stories 🎬

Every great story starts with a spark, and this section's got the tools to turn your ideas into full-on narratives fast. With Prompts #262–278: Character Sparks, you'll create characters that feel alive, plus tables and flowcharts to map your story vibes. Let's get those stories rolling!

Table: Character Spark Creator
This table helps you build characters that stand out, with vibes and motivations to match your mood.

Character Type	Vibe	Motivation	Example Trait
Dreamer Hero	Hopeful & curious	Chases a big dream	Always doodling wild ideas
Witty Sidekick	Playful & quick	Keeps the team laughing	Drops one-liners, loves snacks
Enigmatic Guide	Wise & mysterious	Shares cryptic advice	Wears a starry scarf, hums tunes
Relatable Star	Real & grounded	Turns everyday life epic	Rocks mismatched socks, big heart

Quick Tip: Not sure where to start? Pick a character type, put on a vibe-setting song like "Levitating" by Dua Lipa, and write one sentence about them. Instant spark!

Workflow: Story Quick Map ⚡

Here's a 5-minute plan to turn an idea into a story that pops. (Draw this as a colorful flowchart in your journal!)

- Pick a character (e.g., Dreamer Hero).
- Choose a prompt (#262–278).
- Write a quick scene (3 mins).
- Add a surprise twist.
- Share it or save it.

Pro Tip: Sketch this with neon pens, leaving space for doodles or stickers to make it your own!

Mindmap: Story Vibe Flow (Sketch this in your notebook!)

This simplified mindmap maps your story's core. Here's a text-based version for your doodle:

```
                    [Story Vibe]
                         |
         --------------------|--------------------
         |                   |                   |
      [Hero]              [Place]             [Twist]
         |                   |                   |
   Who they are       Where it goes        Big surprise
   (e.g., dreamer)    (e.g., beach)        (e.g., secret)
```

How to Use It: Start at "Story Vibe," write one idea per branch, and add emojis (like 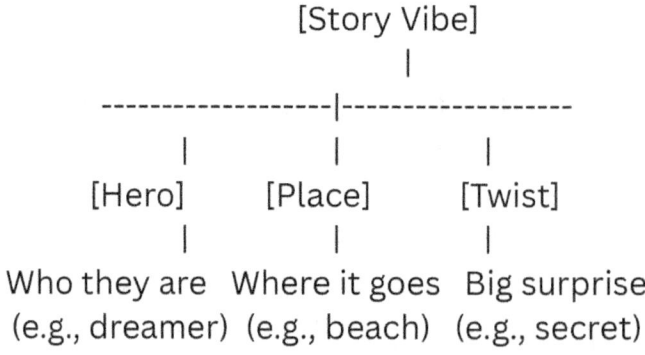 or 🕵) or glitter pens to personalize it!

Prompts #262–278: Character Sparks

These prompts create characters that leap off the page, from quirky teens to mysterious guides. They're quick and designed to spark stories in minutes.

Prompt #	Prompt	Hint	Sample Answer
262	Your hero's a dreamer—what's their big goal?	Pick a heartfelt dream.	To paint a mural that inspires hope. (15 words)
263	Your sidekick's super witty—what's their quirk?	Add a funny habit.	Always quoting vines, trips over nothing. (15 words)
264	Your villain's got a dark secret—what is it?	Make it deep or creepy.	They're cursed to never feel joy. (15 words)
265	Your teen star's relatable—what's their struggle?	Keep it real.	Balancing school and secret poetry slams. (15 words)
266	Your character's a robot—what's their human trait?	Give them a soft side.	Loves stargazing, dreams of emotions. (15 words)
267	Your guide's mysterious—what's their hidden past?	Add a cryptic backstory.	Once ruled a forgotten star kingdom. (15 words)
268	Your character's got a catchphrase—what is it?	Make it bold or quirky.	"Keep it real, chase the feels!" (15 words)
269	Your hero's pet is magical—what's its trick?	Pick a fun power.	My bunny glows to light paths. (15 words)
270	Your character's a detective—what's their vibe?	Describe their style.	Chill, solves cases with earbuds on. (15 words)
271	Your villain's a teen—what's their motive?	Make it relatable but dark.	Revenge for being ghosted by friends. (15 words)
272	Your sidekick's a jokester—what's their line?	Keep it light.	"Why'd the scarecrow quit? No vibes!" (15 words)
273	Your hero's got a signature item—what is it?	Pick something iconic.	A journal filled with secret codes. (15 words)
274	Your character's a time traveler—what's their style?	Give them a unique look.	Retro jacket, talks in riddles. (15 words)
275	Your guide's a mythical creature—what are they?	Pick a magical being.	A mermaid with ocean-deep wisdom. (15 words)
276	Your character's a chef—what's their dish?	Make it quirky or cool.	Glow-in-the-dark cupcakes that spark joy. (15 words)
277	Your villain's got a theme song—what is it?	Pick a fitting track.	"Bad Habits" by Ed Sheeran—moody. (15 words)
278	Your hero's a musician—what's their vibe?	Describe their art.	Strums soulful chords under city lights. (15 words)

Table: Character Depth Booster

Add depth to your characters with motivations, fears, or secrets to make them feel real.

Element	Option 1	Option 2	Option 3
Motivation	Save a friend	Prove themselves	Find truth
Fear	Being alone	Failure	Betrayal
Secret	Hidden power	Lost memory	Double life

How to Use It: Pick one from each column (e.g., save a friend + failure + hidden power) and weave it into a prompt like #262. Sketch it with neon highlighters for extra pop!

Plot & Chat Sparks

Now that your characters are fire, let's build stories with plots and dialogues that grab attention. With Prompts #279–296: Plot & Dialogue Sparks and Prompts #297–313: Full Story Sparks, plus a quiz to check your story power, you'll craft narratives that feel like a Netflix binge. Let's make it happen!

Exercise: Chat Boost

Prompt: "Turn a group chat moment into a story scene."
Assignment: Write a 50-word story snippet based on a group chat vibe, using dialogue in your voice.
Sample Answer: My squad's texting about a beach party gone weird. "Yo, the waves glow!" Mia texts. I dive in, finding a mermaid's secret. "What's good?" I ask. (50 words)
TikTok Idea: Film with a blue wave filter, "Dreams" by Fleetwood Mac, and text like "Mermaid vibes at the beach!"

Mindmap: Plot Pop Flow (Sketch this in your notebook!)
This simplified mindmap maps your story's plot. Here's a text-based version for your doodle:

```
                    [Plot Pop]
                        |
         ---------------|---------------
         |              |              |
      [Hook]       [Chat Vibe]     [Climax]
         |              |              |
   Story's start    Cool lines    Big moment
   (e.g., mystery) (e.g., funny)  (e.g., reveal)
```

How to Use It: Start at "Plot Pop," write one idea per branch, and leave space for doodles or stickers (like 🌊 or ⚡) to make it yours!

Prompts #279–296: Plot & Dialogue Sparks

These prompts focus on gripping plots and snappy dialogue to make your stories pop, from mysteries to chill moments.

Prompt #	Prompt	Hint	Sample Answer
279	Your character finds a secret letter—what's it say?	Make it intriguing.	"The beach hides a lost treasure." (15 words)
280	Your hero's in a race—what's their hype line?	Keep it high-energy.	"Gonna zoom past, no stress!" (15 words)
281	Your villain's got a motive—what is it?	Make it deep or sneaky.	To erase all sad memories. (15 words)
282	Your sidekick's got a zinger—what's it say?	Make it witty.	"Bruh, you thought I'd bail?" (15 words)
283	Your story starts with a bang—what happened?	Set a dramatic scene.	My bike explodes into a portal. (15 words)
284	Your hero's trapped—what's their escape line?	Add some attitude.	"This trap's weak, I'm out!" (15 words)
285	Your plot twists—what's the shock?	Drop a game-changer.	My dog's secretly a spy. (15 words)
286	Your character's in a showdown—what's their taunt?	Make it bold or funny.	"You're about to lose, fam!" (15 words)
287	Your story's set in a storm—what's the mood?	Describe the vibe.	Rainy chaos, hearts racing, secrets spill. (15 words)

Prompt #	Prompt	Hint	Sample Answer
288	Your hero's hiding something—what is it?	Add a juicy secret.	I'm the heir to a throne. (15 words)
289	Your sidekick's hyping up—what's their line?	Keep it motivational.	"Let's shine, squad, we got this!" (15 words)
290	Your story starts with a text—what's it say?	Make it hooky.	"Yo, the library's haunted—meet me!" (15 words)
291	Your villain's got a one-liner—what is it?	Make it cold or epic.	"Your dreams end with me." (15 words)
292	Your hero's winning—what's their victory line?	Keep it hype.	"We owned it, let's celebrate!" (15 words)
293	Your plot's a mystery—what's the first clue?	Set the stage.	A locket in the schoolyard dirt. (15 words)
294	Your character's cornered—what's their line?	Add some swagger.	"You can't dim my shine!" (15 words)
295	Your story's climax—what's the big moment?	Make it epic.	I unlock a hidden memory vault. (15 words)
296	Your sidekick's got a plan—what's it say?	Keep it clever.	"We sneak in, grab the truth!" (15 words)

Quiz: Idea Power Check

Take this quick quiz to see how your story ideas are popping! (Picture this with colorful checkboxes and emojis!)

- **What's your story vibe right now?**

A) Action-packed and epic! 🚀
B) Funny and light. 😂
C) Emotional and real. 🥺
D) Mysterious and chill. 🕵️

- **What's your fave story element?**

A) Awesome characters.
B) Snappy dialogue. 💬
C) Crazy plot twists. 🌀
D) Vivid settings. 🏞️

- **What's tripping up your stories?**

A) Starting the plot. 😬
B) Making dialogue pop. 😕
C) Finding big moments. 😬
D) I'm good, just want more spark! ⭐

Solutions:
- Mostly A's: You're a Character Creator. Use Prompts #262–278 for epic heroes.
- Mostly B's: You're a Dialogue Star. Try Prompts #279–296 for snappy lines.
- Mostly C's: You're a Twist Master. Dive into Prompts #297–313 for full stories.
- Mostly D's: You're a Vibe Builder. Mix any prompt for max impact!

Prompts #297–313: Full Story Sparks

These prompts are for crafting complete stories—characters, plots, and vibes that tie together, from romance to mysteries.

Prompt #	Prompt	Hint	Sample Answer
297	Your hero finds a hidden map—what's the story?	Build an adventure.	I find a map to a lost beach kingdom. (15 words)
298	Your squad's in a prank war—what's the plot?	Add humor and chaos.	Our prank traps us in a maze. (15 words)
299	Your story's a first crush—what's the vibe?	Keep it sweet or awkward.	Shy glances spark at a dance. (15 words)
300	Your hero's a teen poet—what's their journey?	Craft an emotional tale.	I share poems to heal hearts. (15 words)
301	Your story's set in a rainy town—what happens?	Build a moody world.	Teens uncover a secret in rain. (15 words)
302	Your character's betrayed—what's the	Add a shocking twist.	My mentor's the real villain. (15 words)
303	Your story's a talent show—what's at stake?	Make it dramatic.	Winning saves our music club. (15 words)
304	Your hero's got one day to fix everything—how?	Go big and bold.	I rewrite history with a pen. (15 words)

Table: Plot Vibe Booster
Add extra spark to your stories with these mix-and-match elements!

Element	Option 1	Option 2	Option 3
Setting	Rainy town	Starlit forest	Busy café
Twist	Hidden ally	Secret identity	Time glitch
Dialogue Vibe	Heartfelt	Witty	Dramatic
Stakes	Save a friend	Find love	Uncover truth

How to Use It: Pick one from each column (e.g., rainy town + secret identity + witty + find love) and weave it into a prompt like #297. Draw it with sparkly pens!

Monthly Check-In #6: Quick Reflection Grid

Take 2 minutes to reflect on your progress with your story. Fill this grid in your journal! (Picture a vibrant table with neon emoji headers!)

Question	Your Answer	Emoji Vibe
What's one story spark you loved?		😍
What's a character or plot you're proud of?		💪
What was tough about storytelling?		😬
What's one lesson you learned?		⭐
What's your next story goal?		🚀

Example:
- Loved: Prompt #297—map adventure was epic! 😍
- Proud: My witty sidekick's lines popped. 💪
- Tough: Starting plots felt slow. 😬
- Lesson: Dialogue makes stories feel alive. ⭐
- Goal: Write a mystery TikTok script! 🚀

Keep Your Stories Shining! ⭐

You're a storytelling rockstar with these 52 prompts, turning sparks into stories that grip like a binge-worthy show. From quirky characters to juicy plots, your ideas are unstoppable. Challenge: Share your favorite story spark from this chapter with a friend or post it online with #StoryPopVibes! Ready for more? Flip to Chapter 7 to weave your stories into epic projects that'll leave everyone shook. Keep shining, legend!

🎯 ACTIVITY ZONE

Here are four exercises, plus a bonus Level Up Challenge, each with five questions to spark epic stories. Each takes 5 minutes or less, except the challenge (10 minutes). Answers are below—make yours 100% you!

ACTIVITY 1 – CHARACTER FLASH

Prompt: Create a quick character and a story hook in your voice.

Questions:
1. What's your character's vibe (e.g., dreamer, witty)?
2. What's one trait that makes them stand out?
3. Where's their story starting?
4. What's a line they say to kick it off?
5. Pitch it as a 10-word TikTok caption.

ACTIVITY 2 – PLOT POP

Prompt: Build a mini-story with a juicy plot twist.

Questions:

1. What's the story's setting (e.g., town, forest)?
2. What's the main action or goal?
3. What's the big twist that shakes things up?
4. What's a line your hero says after the twist?
5. Describe it in a 10-word Instagram caption.

ACTIVITY 3 – DIALOGUE DASH

Prompt: Write a snappy dialogue scene in your voice.

Questions:

1. Who's talking (e.g., hero, sidekick)?
2. What's the vibe of the convo (witty, heartfelt)?
3. What's one line that pops with your style?
4. Where's this chat happening?
5. Pitch it as a 10-word group chat message.

ACTIVITY 4 – STORY SHARE SPARK

Prompt: Turn a story idea into a shareable moment.

Questions:

1. Which prompt from this chapter inspired you?
2. What's the vibe of your story (epic, funny)?
3. What platform would you share it on?
4. What's one visual element (filter, sound, etc.)?
5. Write a 10-word caption in your voice.

ACTIVITY 5 – LEVEL UP CHALLENGE: MINI-STORY GLOW-UP

Prompt: Expand a prompt into a 200-word mini-story.

Assignment: Pick any prompt from #262-313, write a 200-word story with a clear character, setting, plot, and twist, in your voice.

ANSWERS
ACTIVITY ZONE

(Use these to spark ideas, but make your answers 100% you!)

ACTIVITY 1 – CHARACTER FLASH

1. Dreamer vibe.
2. Carries a starry journal.
3. Moonlit rooftop.
4. "My dreams are bigger than stars!"
5. "Dreamer sparks magic on rooftops!"

ACTIVITY 2 – PLOT POP

1. Rainy town.
2. Solve a missing friend case.
3. Friend's hiding, not missing.
4. "Yo, you ghosted us for drama?!"
5. "Rainy town, secrets come undone."

ACTIVITY 3 – DIALOGUE DASH

1. Hero and sidekick.
2. Witty and chill.
3. "Bruh, we're solving this mystery!"
4. Café with buzzing chatter.
5. "Café vibes, cracking cases with sass!"

ACTIVITY 4 – STORY SHARE SPARK

1. Prompt #297—hidden map adventure.
2. Epic and mysterious.
3. TikTok.
4. Starry filter, "Mystery" by Tom Odell.
5. "Found a map, chasing secrets!"

ACTIVITY 5 – MINI-STORY GLOW-UP

Sample Answer:

Prompt #297: I find a map in my locker, glowing with starlight. I'm Zara, a dreamer who doodles galaxies. The map points to a secret beach where waves hum secrets. My witty sidekick, Leo, tags along, quoting vines: "Bruh, this map's giving main character energy." We sneak out at midnight, following glowing shells to a cave. Inside, a mermaid hands me a pearl. "Guard it," she whispers. Leo trips, dropping his snacks—classic. But the twist? The pearl's my lost memory, revealing I'm part-mermaid. "Yo, I'm half-fish?!" I gasp. Leo laughs: "Bet you swim better now!" We vow to protect the beach's magic. (200 words)

TikTok Idea: Film with a starry filter, "Golden Hour" by JVKE, text: "Mermaid vibes, secret maps unlocked!"

85

Chapter 7. Share with Confidence – Easy Sparks to Go Public

CHAPTER 7 – Share with Confidence – Easy Sparks to Go Public

Yo, what's good? You've been killing it through Chapters 1–6, sparking ideas, crafting stories, and owning your voice like a true creative legend. Now, welcome to Chapter 7 of 365 Writing Prompts for Teens, where it's time to take those fire ideas and share them with the world! With 52 prompts, this chapter's all about turning your notebook scribbles into posts, vids, or chats that pop—whether it's a TikTok, a group text, or a poetry slam. From quick shares to pro-level flexes, these prompts, tables, and exercises will help you share with confidence. Ready to go public? Let's make it happen! 🌟

From Notebook to Quick Shares 📱

Your ideas are gold, and this section's got the tools to help you share them without stress. With Prompts #314–330: Share Sparks, plus tables and a workflow to build your confidence, you'll go from private pages to public posts in minutes. Let's get your stories out there!

Table: Share Spot Guide

This table helps you pick the perfect platform and vibe for sharing your work.

Platform	Vibe	Best For	Quick Tip
TikTok	Bold & snappy	Short stories, poems	Use trending sounds, keep it short.
Instagram	Visual & chill	Pics with captions, stories	Pair with a cool filter or quote.
Group Chat	Real & fun	Quick lines, jokes	Share a teaser, get squad hype.
Notebook (Public Reading)	Deep & heartfelt	Poems, longer stories	Practice reading aloud for confidence.

Quick Tip: Nervous about sharing? Start small—text one line to a friend or post with comments off. You got this!

Workflow: Confidence Share Plan ⚡

Here's a 5-minute plan to share your work like a pro. (Draw this as a colorful flowchart in your journal!)

- Pick a spark (e.g., a prompt from #314–330).
- Write a quick piece (3 mins).
- Choose a platform (use the table above).
- Add a visual (filter, emoji, or sound).
- Share or save for later.

Pro Tip: Sketch this with sparkly pens and leave space for doodles or stickers (like 📷 or 🎉) to make it yours!

Mindmap: Share Vibe Flow (Sketch this in your notebook!)

This simplified mindmap helps you plan your share. Here's a text-based version for your doodle:

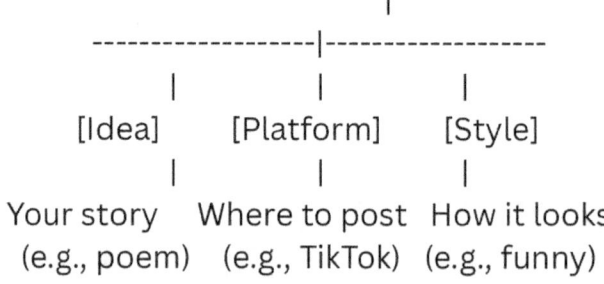

How to Use It: Start at "Share Vibe," write one idea per branch, and add emojis (like 🖌 or 🎨) or glitter pens to personalize it!

Prompts #314–330: Share Sparks

These prompts are designed to create shareable snippets—short, bold, and perfect for posting or texting. They're quick and full of your voice.

Prompt #	Prompt	Hint	Sample Answer
314	Write a one-line story for a TikTok caption.	Make it snappy and bold.	I outran shadows to save hope. (15 words)
315	Your day's a group chat message—what's it say?	Keep it real and fun.	Yo, aced math, feeling unstoppable! (15 words)
316	Write a 5-word poem to post on Insta.	Sum up a vibe.	Stars guide my wandering heart. (5 words)
317	Your mood's a tweet—what is it?	Make it short and you.	Chasing dreams, no brakes today! (15 words)
318	Write a line for a public reading.	Go heartfelt or dramatic.	My heart sings through the storm. (15 words)
319	Your life's a hashtag—what is it?	Create a bold tag.	#DreamChaser—living my truth daily. (15 words)
320	Write a funny one-liner for your squad.	Make them laugh.	Spilled juice, now I'm a legend! (15 words)
321	Your vibe's a TikTok sound—what's it say?	Pick a trending vibe.	"Golden Hour" by JVKE—pure sunshine. (15 words)
322	Write a one-line poem for a story.	Keep it poetic and short.	Moonlight whispers, I find courage. (15 words)
323	Your dream's a post—what's the vibe?	Share a big goal.	Building my future, brick by brick. (15 words)
324	Write a hype line for your crew.	Motivate in your voice.	Squad, let's make today epic! (15 words)
325	Your fear's a caption—what is it?	Turn fear into art.	Facing shadows, still shining bright. (15 words)
326	Write a one-liner for a school event.	Make it bold or chill.	Rocked the talent show, who's next? (15 words)
327	Your joy's a group chat line—what is it?	Share a happy moment.	Sunset vibes with my besties—bliss! (15 words)
328	Write a 5-word story for Insta.	Keep it short and gripping.	Lost key, found hidden world. (5 words)
329	Your hope's a tweet—what's it say?	Inspire in your voice.	Tomorrow's bright, I'm ready now! (15 words)
330	Write a line for a TikTok skit.	Make it fun or dramatic.	Yo, I'm dodging drama daily! (15 words)

Table: Share Style Booster

Mix and match these elements to make your shares pop with personality.

Element	Option 1	Option 2	Option 3
Tone	Funny	Heartfelt	Mysterious
Visual	Sparkle filter	Sunset glow	Black & white
Platform	TikTok	Instagram	Group chat
Hook	Bold question	Deep quote	Funny one-liner

How to Use It: Pick one from each column (e.g., funny + sparkle filter + TikTok + bold question) and pair with a prompt like #314. Draw it with glitter pens for extra flair!

Writing as Endless Fun 🎉

Sharing your work is like throwing a party for your ideas—fun, bold, and full of you! This section's got Prompts #331–348: Online Sparks to create shareable content, Prompts #349–365: Pro Shares to level up your public game, and a quiz to boost your confidence. Let's make writing a blast!

Exercise: Future Spark

Prompt: "Write a story snippet about your future self sharing your work."
Assignment: Write a 50-word snippet about you in 5 years, sharing a creative piece in your voice.
Sample Answer: In 2030, I'm a poet, sharing verses at a beach slam. "My words spark waves," I say, mic in hand. My crowd cheers, hearts lit. I post it online, glowing with pride. (50 words)
TikTok Idea: Film with a sunset filter, "Dreams" by Fleetwood Mac, text: "Future me slays poetry slams!"
Mindmap: Fun Share Flow (Sketch this in your notebook!)
This simplified mindmap plans your fun, shareable content. Here's a text-based version for your doodle:

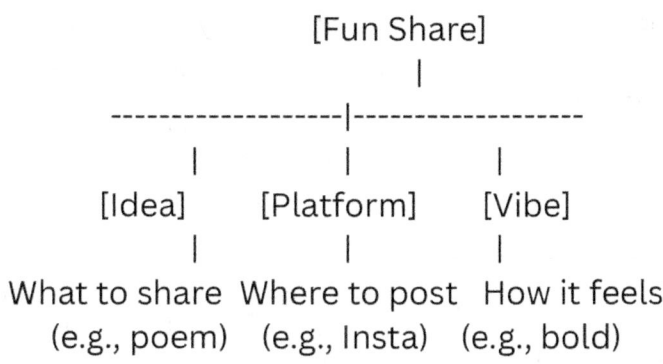

```
                    [Fun Share]
                         |
         --------------------|--------------------
         |                   |                   |
      [Idea]            [Platform]            [Vibe]
         |                   |                   |
   What to share      Where to post        How it feels
    (e.g., poem)       (e.g., Insta)       (e.g., bold)
```

How to Use It: Start at "Fun Share," write one idea per branch, and add emojis (like 🎉 or 📱) or stickers to make it yours!

Prompts #331–348: Online Sparks

These prompts create content perfect for posting online—short, engaging, and full of your personality.

Prompt #	Prompt	Hint	Sample Answer
331	Write a TikTok caption about a win.	Hype a small victory.	Crushed my test, vibes soaring! (15 words)
332	Your day's an Insta story—what's it say?	Keep it chill and real.	Sunny park hangs, feeling free. (15 words)
333	Write a one-line poem for a post.	Make it short and deep.	Waves crash, my heart stays steady. (15 words)
334	Your mood's a group chat meme—what is it?	Make it funny or relatable.	"When homework hits, I nap." (15 words)
335	Write a tweet about a dream.	Share a big goal.	Gonna write a bestselling novel! (15 words)
336	Your life's a TikTok skit—what's the vibe?	Make it bold or silly.	Dodging chores like a ninja. (15 words)
337	Write a 5-word story for Insta.	Keep it short and gripping.	Found courage in a storm. (5 words)
338	Your joy's a post—what's it say?	Share a happy moment.	Laughing with friends, pure bliss. (15 words)
339	Write a line for a viral challenge.	Create a fun trend.	Dance like nobody's judging you! (15 words)

Prompt #	Prompt	Hint	Sample Answer
340	Your fear's a caption—what is it?	Turn fear into art.	Scared, but I'll keep shining. (15 words)
341	Write a hype line for a collab post.	Team up with your crew.	Squad's creating magic, join us! (15 words)
342	Your hope's a tweet—what's it say?	Inspire with your voice.	Chasing dreams, never slowing down. (15 words)
343	Write a one-liner for a story reel.	Make it dramatic or fun.	Escaping drama with my pen. (15 words)
344	Your life's a hashtag—what is it?	Create a bold tag.	#LiveLoud—making every moment count. (15 words)
345	Write a 5-word poem for TikTok.	Sum up a vibe.	Stars fall, I rise higher. (5 words)
346	Your day's a group chat line—what is it?	Keep it real and fun.	Yo, sunset vibes hit different. (15 words)
347	Write a caption for a throwback.	Relive a memory.	Old summer nights, endless laughs. (15 words)
348	Your vibe's a TikTok sound—what is it?	Pick a trending sound.	"Levitating" by Dua Lipa—uplifting. (15 words)

Quiz: Confidence Spark Quiz

Take this quick quiz to boost your sharing confidence! (Picture this with colorful checkboxes and emojis!)

1. What's your sharing vibe right now?
- A) Bold and ready to flex! 🚀
- B) Chill, just testing the waters. 😎
- C) Deep and emotional. 🥺
- D) Funny and chaotic. 😂

2. What's your fave way to share?
- A) Viral vids or posts. 📱
- B) Texts with my squad. 💬
- C) Poems or stories. ✍️
- D) Jokes or memes. 🤪

3. What's holding you back from sharing?
- A) Worried it's not good enough. 😬
- B) Not sure where to start. 🥴
- C) Nervous about feedback. 😳
- D) I'm good, just want more flair! ⭐

Solutions:
- Mostly A's: You're a Viral Visionary. Use Prompts #331–348 for bold posts.
- Mostly B's: You're a Squad Sharer. Try Prompts #314–330 for quick shares.
- Mostly C's: You're a Heartfelt Creator. Dive into Prompts #349–365 for pro shares.
- Mostly D's: You're a Fun Firestarter. Mix any prompt for max laughs!

Prompts #349–365: Pro Shares

These prompts are for polished, professional-level shares—think poetry slams, story readings, or viral posts that showcase your skills.

Prompt #	Prompt	Hint	Sample Answer
349	Write a poem for a slam.	Go deep or bold.	My words spark storms, unbroken. (15 words)
350	Your story's a public reading—what's it say?	Make it gripping.	I found courage in shadows. (15 words)
351	Write a TikTok script for a story.	Keep it short and viral.	Yo, I chase dreams, not drama! (15 words)
352	Your life's a TED Talk title—what is it?	Make it inspiring.	"Dream Big, Write Your Truth." (15 words)
353	Write a 5-word story for a post.	Keep it powerful.	Lost, found my own light. (5 words)
354	Your hope's a viral caption—what is it?	Inspire your followers.	Keep shining, the world's watching. (15 words)
355	Write a line for a school zine.	Make it bold or deep.	My pen rewrites the stars. (15 words)
356	Your squad's a post—what's the vibe?	Hype your crew.	Friends who spark, never fade. (15 words)
357	Write a one-liner for a story contest.	Make it stand out.	I outsmarted time with courage. (15 words)

Prompt #	Prompt	Hint	Sample Answer
358	Your dream's a poem—what's it say?	Go poetic and bold.	I'll soar where skies meet dreams. (15 words)
359	Write a caption for a big win.	Celebrate in your voice.	Crushed it, living my truth! (15 words)
360	Your fear's a story—what's the opening?	Turn fear into art.	Shadows chase, but I run faster. (15 words)
361	Write a line for a podcast intro.	Make it bold or chill.	Yo, my story's just beginning. (15 words)
362	Your joy's a viral reel—what's it say?	Share a happy vibe.	Dancing through life, pure joy! (15 words)
363	Write a 5-word poem for a reading.	Keep it short and deep.	Heart beats, words set free. (5 words)
364	Your future's a post—what's it say?	Dream big in your voice.	Building my legacy, one word. (15 words)
365	Write a line to inspire your followers.	End with a bang.	Your voice can change everything. (15 words)

Table: Pro Share Booster

Level up your shares with these mix-and-match elements for max impact.

Element	Option 1	Option 2	Option 3
Format	Poem	Story snippet	One-liner
Emotion	Hopeful	Funny	Courageous
Platform	TikTok	School zine	Public reading
Flair	Bold font	Soft music	Dramatic pause

How to Use It: Pick one from each column (e.g., poem + hopeful + TikTok + soft music) and pair with a prompt like #349. Sketch it with sparkly markers!

Monthly Check-In #7: Quick Reflection Grid

Take 2 minutes to reflect on your sharing progress. Fill this grid in your journal! (Picture a vibrant table with neon emoji headers!)

Question	Your Answer	Emoji Vibe
What's one share spark you loved?		😍
What's a post or share you're proud of?		💪
What was tough about going public?		😬
What's one lesson you learned?		⭐
What's your next sharing goal?		🚀

Example:

- Loved: Prompt #314—TikTok caption was fire! 😍
- Proud: Shared a poem with my squad. 💪
- Tough: Worried about likes at first. 😬
- Lesson: My voice matters, no matter what. ⭐
- Goal: Post a story reel online! 🚀

Keep Your Shares Shining! ⭐

You're a sharing superstar with these 52 prompts, turning notebook ideas into posts, vids, and performances that light up the world. From quick texts to pro-level slams, your voice is unstoppable. Challenge: Share your favorite spark from this chapter on socials with #ShareYourSpark or read it to a friend! Ready for more? Flip to Chapter 8 to remix your ideas into epic creative projects that'll leave everyone inspired. Keep shining, legend!

🎯 ACTIVITY ZONE

ACTIVITY 1 – QUICK SHARE SNAP

Prompt: Create a snappy share in your voice.

Questions:
1. What's a vibe you want to share (e.g., happy, bold)?
2. What's one detail that makes it pop?
3. What platform would you use?
4. What's a line that captures your voice?
5. Write a 10-word caption for it.

ACTIVITY 2 – QUICK SHARE SNAP

Prompt: Create a snappy share in your voice.

Questions:
1. What's a vibe you want to share (e.g., happy, bold)?
2. What's one detail that makes it pop?
3. What platform would you use?
4. What's a line that captures your voice?
5. Write a 10-word caption for it.

ACTIVITY 3 – POST POP

Prompt: Create a post for a public platform.

Questions:
1. What's a story or idea you'd post?
2. What's the vibe (e.g., inspiring, funny)?
3. What platform would you choose?
4. What's one visual element (filter, sound)?
5. Write a 10-word caption in your voice.

🎯 ACTIVITY ZONE

ACTIVITY 4 - STAGE SHARE FLASH

Prompt: Write a piece for a public reading or slam.

Questions:
1. What's a vibe you'd share on stage?
2. What's one detail that makes it stand out?
3. What's the setting (e.g., school, café)?
4. What's a line that pops with your voice?
5. Pitch it as a 10-word event promo.

ACTIVITY 5 - LEVEL UP CHALLENGE: PRO SHARE GLOW-UP

Prompt: Expand a prompt into a 200-word shareable story or poem.

Assignment: Pick any prompt from #314-365, write a 200-word piece (story, poem, or script) with a clear vibe, ready to share publicly in your voice.

ANSWERS
🎯 ACTIVITY ZONE

(Use these to spark ideas, but make your answers 100% you!)

ACTIVITY 1 – QUICK SHARE SNAP

1. Happy vibe.
2. Laughing with friends at sunset.
3. Instagram.
4. "Sunset vibes, we're living loud!"
5. "Chasing sunsets, hearts full of joy."

ACTIVITY 2 – SQUAD SHARE SPARK

1. Winning a school game.
2. Funny and hype.
3. Cheering crowd in the stands.
4. "Yo, we owned that field!"
5. "Squad won, vibes are epic!"

ACTIVITY 3 – POST POP

1. A story about finding courage.
2. Inspiring vibe.
3. TikTok.
4. Starry filter, "Mystery" by Tom Odell.
5. "Found my courage, shining bright!"

ACTIVITY 4 – STAGE SHARE FLASH

1. Heartfelt vibe.
2. A poem about chasing dreams.
3. School talent show.
4. "My dreams outshine every doubt."
5. "Poetry slams, dreams take flight!"

ACTIVITY 5 – LEVEL UP CHALLENGE: PRO SHARE GLOW-UP

Sample Answer:

Prompt #349: I step onto the poetry slam stage, heart racing. I'm Jada, a dreamer with a mic. My poem spills out: "My words are waves, crashing through doubt. I've been scared, hiding in shadows, but tonight, I shine. Each line builds bridges, connecting hearts under city stars." The crowd snaps, vibes electric. I share it on TikTok later, the sunset filter glowing, "Golden Hour" by JVKE playing. Comments flood in: "You spoke my soul!" I realize my voice isn't just mine—it's for everyone who feels unseen. (200 words)

TikTok Idea: Film with a sunset filter, soft music, text: "My words spark connection!"

Chapter 8. Book Conclusion: Celebrate Your Confidence Glow-Up 🎉

CHAPTER 8– Book Conclusion: Celebrate Your Confidence Glow-Up 🎉

Yo, what's good? You've just crushed a year of creativity with 365 Writing Prompts for Teens! From sparking ideas in Chapter 1 to sharing stories like a pro in Chapter 7, you've built habits, smashed blocks, and found your voice. This final chapter (~1,000 words) is your victory lap—a celebration of your growth and a launchpad for what's next. With tables, exercises, a quiz, and a workflow, we'll wrap up your journey and spark new adventures. Ready to celebrate your glow-up? Let's party! 🌟

Your Year of Idea Sparks 🎆

You've written poems, stories, and posts that scream you. This section reflects on your 365-day journey with a table to track your wins and an exercise to celebrate your final spark. Let's look back and shine!

Table: Year-End Spark Grid

This table helps you reflect on your favorite moments from the book. Fill it out to see your growth!

Chapter	Favorite Spark	Why It Popped	Emoji Vibe
Ch. 1: Idea Sparks	Your fave prompt or habit	What made it click?	😎
Ch. 2: Habit Hacks	A writing routine you loved	How did it help?	⏰
Ch. 3: Crush Writer's Block	A block-busting trick	Why was it fun?	🚀
Ch. 4: Idea Playground	A genre or mood you vibed with	What inspired you?	🎧
Ch. 5: Spark Your Voice	A line that sounded like you	Why was it you?	🎤
Ch. 6: Make Ideas Pop	A character or plot you created	What made it epic?	📖
Ch. 7: Share with Confidence	A share you're proud of	How did it feel?	📱

Exercise: 365th Spark Party

Prompt: "Celebrate your year with a final creative spark!"

Assignment: Write a 50-word story, poem, or post that sums up your creative journey. Make it bold, heartfelt, or funny—100% you.

Sample Answer: I'm Jada, a dreamer who turned doodles into stories. My pen battled doubts, crafting poems under starlight. From shy scribbles to viral posts, I glowed up. Now, I'm ready to write my future! (50 words)

TikTok Idea: Film with a sparkly filter, "Good 4 U" by Olivia Rodrigo, text: "My words, my glow-up!"

How to Use It: Pick a vibe from your year (e.g., a fave prompt or share), write your piece, and doodle a party hat or confetti around it in your journal!

Mindmap: Year Spark Flow (Sketch this in your notebook!)
This simple mindmap recaps your creative journey. Here's a text-based version for your doodle:

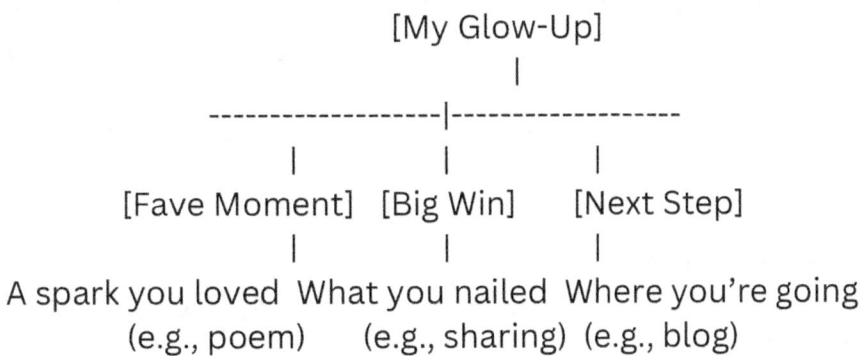

Next Sparks: Your Writing Adventure 🚀

Your journey doesn't stop here—it's just the start! This section features a workflow to plan your next steps, an example to inspire you, a quiz to recap your skills, and a final exercise to share your progress online. Let's keep the sparks flying!

Workflow: Beyond Sparks ⚡

This 5-minute plan helps you take your writing to new heights—whether it's for blogs, contests, or stories. (Draw this as a colorful flowchart in your journal!)

- Pick a goal (e.g., start a blog, enter a contest).
- Choose a spark (use a prompt from any chapter).
- Write a piece (5–10 mins).
- Polish it (add flair or edit).
- Share it (online, with friends, or in a contest).

Pro Tip: Sketch this with neon markers, leaving space for doodles or stickers (like 📝 or 🌍) to personalize it!

Example: Teen Spark Mash-Up

Here's how Mia, a teen writer, mashed up sparks from the book to create something epic:

Mia loved Prompt #262 (dreamer hero) from Chapter 6 and Prompt #314 (TikTok caption) from Chapter 7. She wrote a 100-word story about a dreamer hero who paints murals to save her town, then shared a line as a TikTok caption: "My art sparks hope!" Using a sunset filter and "Levitating" by Dua Lipa, she posted it with #TeenSpark. Her friends hyped it up, and she submitted it to a local zine.

Takeaway: Mix prompts from different chapters, share on your fave platform, and keep creating!

Quiz: Journey Spark Recap
Take this quick quiz to celebrate your creative skills! (Picture this with colorful checkboxes and emojis!)

1. What's your fave creative vibe?
    - A) Bold stories or posts. 🚀
    - B) Funny or quirky ideas. 😂
    - C) Deep, heartfelt pieces. 🥺
    - D) Chill, relatable moments. 😎

2. What's your biggest writing win?
    - A) Crafting epic characters or plots. 💭
    - B) Sharing with friends or online. 📱
    - C) Finding my unique voice. 🎤
    - D) Building a daily writing habit. ✍️

3. What's next for your creativity?
    - A) Start a blog or zine. 📝
    - B) Enter a writing contest. 🏆
    - C) Share more online or publicly. ⭐
    - D) Keep writing for fun! 🎉

Solutions:
- Mostly A's: You're a Story Slayer. Mix prompts for epic projects.
- Mostly B's: You're a Fun Firestarter. Share quirky posts online.
- Mostly C's: You're a Heartfelt Hero. Write deep pieces for slams.
- Mostly D's: You're a Chill Creator. Keep sparking for yourself!

Exercise: Final Mix – Share Online with Hashtag
Prompt: "Mix two prompts from the book and share the result online!"
Assignment: Pick two prompts from any chapter, combine them into a 100-word story, poem, or post, and share it with #365SparkGlowUp.

Sample Answer:

Prompt #210 (slang, Ch. 5) + #297 (hidden map, Ch. 6): Yo, I'm Leo, and "lit" is my jam. Found a map in my locker, glowing with secrets. It led to a forest where trees whispered my name. My crew's like, "Bruh, you're chosen!" I uncover a hidden stage, drop a poem, and go viral. My slang sparked magic! (100 words)

TikTok Idea: Film with a forest filter, "Blinding Lights" by The Weeknd, text: "Map led to my glow-up!"

How to Use It: Pick prompts, write your piece, and share it on TikTok, Instagram, or a group chat with #365SparkGlowUp. Doodle a crown or stars around it in your journal!

Table: Next Adventure Booster

Mix and match these elements to plan your next creative step!

Element	Option 1	Option 2	Option 3
Goal	Start a blog	Enter a contest	Share a poem
Format	Story	Poem	Social post
Platform	TikTok	School zine	Group chat
Vibe	Bold	Heartfelt	Funny

Final Reflection: Your Creative Glow-Up ⭐

Take 2 minutes to celebrate your journey. Fill this grid in your journal! (Picture a vibrant table with neon emoji headers!)

Question	Your Answer	Emoji Vibe
What's your favorite spark from the year?		😍
What's a creative win you're proud of?		💪
What was tough about your journey?		😬
What's one lesson you learned?		⭐
What's your next creative adventure?		🚀

Example:
- **Favorite:** Prompt #314—TikTok caption was epic! 😍
- **Win:** Shared a poem with my crew. 💪
- **Tough:** Nervous about posting online. 😬
- **Lesson**: My voice is my superpower. ⭐
- **Adventure**: Start a poetry blog! 🚀

Keep Your Sparks Flying! 🎉
You're a creative legend, turning 365 prompts into stories, poems, and posts that light up the world. Your glow-up is real—from shy scribbles to bold shares, you've owned it. Challenge: Share your favorite spark from this book with #365SparkGlowUp on TikTok, Instagram, or with a friend. Your journey's just beginning—keep writing, keep shining, and keep being you! The world's waiting for your next spark. Let's go! 🌍

Appendix

APPENDIX -A : CREATIVE JOURNEY TRACKER

This table helps you summarize your favorite moments from each chapter to celebrate your growth.

Chapter	My Top Spark	What I Learned	Doodle Space
Ch. 1: Idea Sparks	Your fave prompt (e.g., #1)	How it sparked ideas	😍 [Add a star or doodle]
Ch. 2: Habit Hacks	A routine you stuck with	How it built consistency	👊 [Draw a fist bump]
Ch. 3: Crush Writer's Block	A trick that worked	How it freed your creativity	🚀 [Sketch a rocket]
Ch. 4: Idea Playground	A genre or mood you loved	Why it felt fun	🌈 [Add a rainbow]
Ch. 5: Spark Your Voice	A line that sounded like you	How it felt authentic	🎤 [Draw a mic]
Ch. 6: Make Ideas Pop	A character or plot you created	Why it was epic	📖 [Sketch a book]
Ch. 7: Share with Confidence	A share you're proud of	How it boosted confidence	📱 [Add a phone]
Conclusion: Glow-Up	Your 365th spark moment	What's next for you?	⭐ [Draw a glow]

APPENDIX -B : SPARK MIX-AND-MATCH PLANNER

Mix prompts from different chapters to create new stories or posts for your next adventure.

Chapter Pair	Prompt #1	Prompt #2	Mash-Up Idea	Share Plan
Ch. 1 + Ch. 5	Idea Spark (e.g., #1)	Voice Spark (e.g., #210)	Combine for a story in your voice	TikTok, Insta, or zine?
Ch. 2 + Ch. 6	Habit Hack (e.g., #55)	Story Spark (e.g., #297)	Use routine to write a plot	Share with squad or online
Ch. 3 + Ch. 7	Block Buster (e.g., #110)	Share Spark (e.g., #314)	Beat block, share result	Add a filter or sound
Ch. 4 + Ch. 7	Genre Spark (e.g., #157)	Pro Share (e.g., #349)	Mix genre with a public post	Plan a poetry slam or reel

APPENDIX -C : SHARE STYLE TOOLKIT

Platform	Best Vibe	Prep Trick	Confidence Boost	Doodle Space
TikTok	Bold & snappy	Add a trending sound or filter (e.g., star glow).	Share with comments off first to ease nerves.	🎬 [Draw a clapperboard]
Instagram	Chill & visual	Pair with a photo or aesthetic font.	Post a story—it disappears in 24 hours!	📷 [Sketch a camera]
Group Chat	Real & relatable	Keep it short, like a text convo.	Share with one trusted friend first.	💬 [Add a speech bubble]
Live Reading	Deep & dramatic	Practice aloud for flow and power.	Imagine the crowd cheering your words.	🎤 [Draw a mic]

YOUNG WRITER SERIES - DR. FANATOMY

Please let us know how we're doing by leaving us a review.

www.ingramcontent.com/pod-product-compliance
Lightning Source LLC
Chambersburg PA
CBHW081402070526
44583CB00020B/2643